P

From:

Date:

Why
Jesus
Appears
to People Today

A Biblical Understanding

Why Jesus Appears

to People Today

A Biblical Understanding

MEL BOND

DESTINY IMAGE® PUBLISHERS, INC.
P.O. Box 310, Shippensburg, PA 17257-0310
"Promoting Inspired Lives."

This book and all other Destiny Image, Revival Press, MercyPlace, Fresh Bread, Destiny Image Fiction, and Treasure House books are available at Christian bookstores and distributors worldwide.

For a U.S. bookstore nearest you, call 1-800-722-6774.
For more information on foreign distributors, call 717-532-3040.
Reach us on the Internet: www.destinyimage.com.

ISBN 13 TP: 978-0-7684-4117-8
ISBN 13 Ebook: 978-0-7684-8844-9

For Worldwide Distribution, Printed in the U.S.A.
1 2 3 4 5 6 7 8 / 16 15 14 13 12

DEDICATION

I dedicate this book to my mother, Anna Marie (Bray) Robey, who was born February 5, 1929 in her father's and mother's home on Ridge Road back in the woods of Troy, Missouri.

At the age of 13, she accepted the Lord Jesus as her personal Savior, was baptized in water in the Merrimac River, and was filled with the Holy Spirit with the evidence of speaking in tongues.

After my father, Eleven Lee Bond, returned home from being in World War II he was in the infantry and received a purple heart for being wounded in battle, a bronze star for heroic action in battle, and four bronze stars for being in the Battle of the Bulge, Normandy Beach Head, and Anzio Beach Head.

My mother and father married August 2, 1947 and raised five children: Carolyn, myself, Larry, Rhonda, and Susan.

I have very fond memories of the great love and dedication that my mother had and still has for the Lord. She was the greatest foundation for me and my siblings in accepting the Lord and living good Christian lives.

She has placed deposits of the rich goodness of the Lord in my life that will be there throughout eternity.

Before she ever conceived me, she told me that she had prayed for a boy. Her prayers have been a major part of who I am today.

My father went on to be with the Lord August 13, 2004. And my mother still lives a rich Christian life and is really a legend.

I am extremely blessed to have a mother who has put such rich qualities in my life and the lives of all of my siblings.

It would really take a book to do justice to my mother for the great life she has lived.

Thank you, Mom,

Mel Bond

CONTENTS

FOREWORD

I am honored to have been asked to write the foreword for this book, *Why Jesus Appears to People*. I have personally known the author, Mel Bond, for about 20 years. It has been my privilege to minister to his congregation. For as long as I have known Mel, he has had an awareness of the supernatural.

Noah Webster's Dictionary of 1828 defines *supernatural* in this manner:

Second Kings 6:1-7. Being beyond or exceeding the powers of laws of nature; miraculous. A supernatural event is one which is not produced according to the ordinary or established laws of natural things. Thus if iron has a more specific gravity than water, it will sink in that fluid; and the floating of iron on water must be a supernatural event. Now no human being can alter the law of nature; the floating of iron on water therefore must be caused by divine power.

There are various ways our Lord appears to His followers. The way the Lord appears to one person may differ from way He appears to another—but He will appear.

For your benefit, I offer additional definitions from Noah Webster's Dictionary of 1828. Mr. Webster was a very God-fearing follower of our Lord Jesus. His definitions of the various ways our Lord has and can appear to you are beneficial.

The definition of *dream*:

The thought or series of thoughts of a person in sleep. We apply dream, in the singular, to a series of thoughts, which occupy the mind of a sleeping person, in which he imagines he has a view of real things or transactions. In scripture, dreams were sometimes impressions on the minds of sleeping persons made by divine agency. God came to Abimelech in a dream. Joseph was warned by God in a dream. Genesis 20 and Matthew 2.

The definition of *vision*:

The act of seeing external objects; actual sight. Faith here is turned into sight there. In scripture, a revelation from God; an appearance or exhibition of something supernaturally presented to the prophets, by which they were informed of future events. Such were the visions of Isaiah, of Amos, of Ezekiel, etc.

The definition of *appearance*:

The act of coming into sight; the act of becoming visible to the eye; as his sudden appearance surprised me. Semblance; apparent likeness. There was upon the tabernacle as it were the appearance of Fire. Numbers 9.

One who enjoys reading will find this book interesting and challenging. I pray it will cause you to more thoroughly research and study the magnificent Word of the Living God.

Hilton Sutton, Th.D.

PREFACE

In this book I will show from the Scriptures why Jesus appears to people and the purpose of Him appearing to people.

By reading this book you will also understand from the Scriptures how Jesus wants to appear to everyone and how a person can get into the position for Jesus to appear to them.

I will also tell you about a few times that Jesus appeared to me and the things I learned from the experiences. I give these experience to show you: first, the importance of Jesus appearing to a person and how it changes your life supernaturally. Second, to show you the different ways Jesus appears to people.

I have never prayed or desired for Jesus to appear to me. I believe based upon sound Scriptures that the reason Jesus has appeared to me so many times is the fact that I have put God's Word in such a high priority in my life.

Why Jesus Appears to People Today

June 17, 1958 was a very important day in my life. It was a Tuesday and about 10 o'clock in the morning. I was by myself at home because the rest of the family went somewhere and I did not want to go. We lived on Annapolis Street in Overland, Missouri. I walked into my mother's and father's bedroom, and as soon as I walked into the bedroom I sensed that I needed to know God in a personal way; I needed Him in my life. I was seven years old at that time but had the same perception that I do now. Children know there is something missing in their life without Jesus being the Lord of their life. In John 10:10 Jesus said, "I am come to give life and give it more abundantly." A person who has not been born again knows there is something of great importance missing in their life.

Job 32:8 says, "But there is a spirit in man: and the inspiration of the Almighty giveth them understanding." Note: the word *inspiration* is the Hebrew word *nshamah*. This word is coequally rendered as: vital *breath*, divine *inspiration*.

Every human being has an eternal, supernatural spirit in them and that spirit must have vital breath, divine inspiration from God, or they will live a life that is empty and live in a lost state. They will always be looking for something to fulfill that lost state. They actually have a dead spirit and that is why they are always seeking for something to give them more life, only to have greater disappointment and emptiness in their life. Only God can give real life, when a person accepts Jesus Christ as their Lord and Savior (see Rom.10:9-10).

I looked at my mother's and father's bed which had a

white chenille bed spread with light purple figures of swans on it. I knelt down and put my face into my hands, crying. I ask Jesus to be the Lord of my life. I told Him I wanted all of Him; and then I began speaking in tongues, God's heavenly language (see Acts 2:4).

I was a different young boy. I would get a group of kids together from the neighborhood there on Annapolis Street in Overland, Missouri and would get my Bible and tell the kids about the goodness of God.

Within a few weeks I was in church. My mother always took us to church, but the pastor did not always have an altar call for people to be saved (born again). However, I was always ready to follow the pattern taught in the church, which was, the pastor would preach his sermon and then have the people close their eyes and raise their hands if they wanted to be saved (born again).

So when the time came, I was ready to do this in church. We went to a very successful Full Gospel church in the St. Louis, Missouri area, so I thought that I needed to do this the way the church teaches for this to be really valid. So when the time came, the pastor finished his sermon and asked everyone to bow their heads and close their eyes. Then he asked if there was anyone who needed to be saved, and that they would go to hell if they were not. I do not remember everything the pastor preached, as my focus was to validate my salvation experience that I received at home, because I never heard of anyone ever getting saved at home.

So after the pastor finished his sermon, I closed my eyes and lifted my right hand. I purposely sat about three seats from the front on the very end of the seat, right next to the aisle, prepared to come forward for salvation. It seemed like a long time of having my hand up. Finally, I noticed someone grab my face with their right hand very rough. I looked and it was the pastor. He then put his mouth to my right ear and said, "You're just a stupid little kid and you do not know what you're doing; put your hand down."

I will never forget those words, as they were words of torture, of death. My family was a poor family. There were five of us kids and we wore patches on our clothes. In those days wearing patches was a disgrace. My mother always made sure we were clean, our clothes were clean, but we wore patches and patches most definitely were not cool in those days. We were considered the outcasts. And then what made it worse was the fact that my mother and father both had American Indian blood, so all of us kids were dark-haired with dark skin. The kids at school would call me *mulatto*. So I was not a banker, a lawyer, or some refined-looking prize for this pastor to have come to the altar. I would say this pastor was ashamed to have my family in his church.

So this was a major turning point in my life. I started believing that there was no such thing as God. How could there be? One of the most successful pastors in St. Louis proved to me there was no God. I always thought this pastor must know God more than most of the people in the world, as he is one of the most successful pastors in one of the largest cities in the world. I figured if this was God's man, then I did not want anything to do with God.

So little by little satan worked his way in my life. By the time I was 14 years old I was involved with a bad motorcycle gang. I was involved in drugs and heavy street fighting, and the list goes on. I literally had demons that would use me to fulfill evil. I would fight always with the intent to kill. I really do not like to think or talk about the lifestyle that I had, as the Lord has given me real life and a new heart and a new mind. At home, most of the time my family did not know of the double lifestyle that I lived.

By the time I was 16 years of age I had attempted suicide two times. I should have died both times but did not. So I signed up for the Marine Corp for four years, as they promised me that I would go to Vietnam. My plans were to run out in front of the enemy, firing my weapon, and they would shoot me dead. However, the Marine Corps told me they could not take me until I was 17 for a couple of months, as that was their policy for enlisting at that time. After about a week, I was very frustrated, so I went to the Army recruiter and asked them how soon they could take me. They told me I could be in the day after I turned 17. So I signed up for the Army for three years in 1967. I was sent to Korea for about 14 months and had some real life-changing experiences there in Pusan, Korea and things straightened out in my life. I wondered if I would have to go into the Marine Corps after I finished my three years enlistment with the Army, but it never happened.

Once I was in the Army, I signed up for AirBorne and anything else that would promise to get me to Vietnam. However, once I was in, I found out that I was given the wrong information. The military would not allow soldiers to go to Vietnam until they were at least 18 years of age. So they sent me to South Korea. I was really a very miserable person.

I was stationed at Pusan Base Command on guard duty. One night, it was about 2 A.M. and I was miserable. I looked up into the heavens and began to cry. I said, "If there is a God, prove yourself to me, and I will live for You!" I put my head down weeping for only a few moments when I heard something over the top of my head that sounded like a bird flying close by. I looked up and I saw the most beautiful white dove that was glowing and flying in place about 10 feet directly over my head. I remembered the Sunday school lessons and I knew the Holy Spirit came in the form of a dove over the top of Jesus' head when He was being baptized in water. Then I watched the dove fly about 30 feet away and vanish in front of my eyes. I knew this was the Holy Spirit. I knew this was God proving to me that He was real.

From that moment I began reading my little New Testament, given to me by my father, who had carried it with him all through World War II. I read that little New Testament six times the first year after this experience; I also memorized about 100 to 200 verses that same year.

From that time on I have continued to read and memorize the Word of God in a very daily and dedicated manner. I did not read and memorize the Bible to try and prove anything to anyone. I did not do it to prepare for the ministry. I did it to save my life! It delivered me from the torment of satan and gave me peace, joy, satisfaction, and peace of mind, which I had never had since that July 17 morning in my mother's and father's bedroom.

I was unknowingly fulfilling a scriptural foundation for Jesus to appear to a person. As you study this book you will find when one puts God's Word in their spirit, mind, and life this causes a person to get into a position for Jesus to appear to them. A major key for Jesus appearing to people is the Word of God in one's spirit and mind.

He that hath My commandments, and keepeth them, he it is that loveth Me: and he that loveth Me shall be loved of My Father, and I will love him, and will **manifest** *Myself to him* (John 14:21).

The Greek word for *manifest* in this verse is *emphanizo*. This word is coequally rendered as "to exhibit (in person), appear (plainly), and show."

In the first chapter of this book I give you Scriptures that validate why Jesus appears to people and you will find that they correlate with my experience of giving God's Word such strong prominence in my life.

I will also share nine different experiences of Jesus appearing to me. I am sure the Lord has appeared to me more than the nine times. However, these are the ones the Lord has brought to my attention to put in this book. The purpose of sharing these different experiences is so you can know that Jesus still appears to common people today and that He appears in many different ways. You will also learn that visions can give confirmation to God's Word, which will help you go into deeper truths.

I realize God's Word stands alone and does not need any support or confirmation. However, as you study about Jesus appearing to Thomas in John 20:25-29, you will notice that Thomas said he would not believe until he saw. Jesus came to Thomas's level and appeared to him and let him feel His hands and His person.

I was like Thomas. After the negative experience with the pastor, I had to see, because it was hard for me to believe there was a God. God is a loving God, and He will come to our level.

A major reason for this book is to teach the simplicity of Jesus appearing to people. Through my observations in the ministry since the age of 17 and in a full-time position of ministry since 1972, I've noticed a very scriptural truth—people will do what they are taught. Some churches do not teach about the supernatural experience of being filled with the Holy Spirit and speaking in tongues, and nobody speaks in tongues in those churches. The same is true of healings, miracles, and all of the gifts of the Holy Spirit and prosperity. I've seen some very large churches in which most of the people have horrible financial problems because people are not taught the many truths of God's Word such as Psalm 35:27: "Let the Lord be magnified, which hath pleasure in the prosperity of His servant." (Keep in mind today we are not servants, we are His children! How much more ought His children to be prosperous).

So, if people are not taught that Jesus wants to appear to them, they do not have visitations of Jesus.

This book will help get you into a position to have your

life supernaturally changed by Jesus appearing to you again and again!

Note: I fully promote God's Word as final authority, knowing that there is not any type of a vision or a literal manifestation of Jesus, an angel, or any other supernatural manifestation to be exalted or promoted above God's Word. God's Word is the final authority.

But though we, or an angel from heaven, preach any other gospel unto you than that which we have preached unto you, let him be accursed (Galatians 1:8).

CHAPTER 1

Why Jesus Appears to People

Because of the Word

The Bible teaches that if we love God we will keep His commandments, and then He will love us and appear to us.

Read John 14:21 again: "He that hath My commandments, and keepeth them, he it is that loveth Me: and he that loveth Me shall be loved of My Father, and I will love him, and will manifest Myself to him."

Note that the commandments of God are the Words of God: First Corinthians 14:37, "...the things that I write unto you are the commandments of the Lord." First John 2:7, "Brethren, I write no new commandment unto you, but an old commandment which ye had from the beginning. The old commandment is the word which ye have heard from the beginning." First John 3:23, "And this is His commandment, That we should believe on the name of His Son Jesus Christ, and love one another, as He gave us commandment."

The phrase, "Him, and will manifest" in John 14:21 is one Greek word: *emphanizō*. As mentioned in the Introduction, this word is translated as: to *exhibit* (in person), appear, declare (plainly), manifest, shew. Plainly, if we love God's Word, Jesus will exhibit in person; He will appear to us!

At the age of 17, I recommitted my life to the Lord. I had a lot of problems from the past and demonic thoughts tried to rule my life. So I read the New Testament at least six times that year and memorized about 100 to 200 verses. I also read the Old Testament once. I did these things not to try to impress anyone, nor to prepare for the ministry. I had no thoughts of going into the ministry at this time. I read the Word of God and memorized it to give me peace of mind and happiness in my life—as well as to give me power over sin and the torments of the devil.

And it did that. The more I read and memorized the Word of God, the better my life got; the more peace and happiness came into my life. So I continued to follow this pattern even to this day. And I am convinced this is the major reason Jesus has appeared to me many times and why I have had spiritual experiences—because I love the Word and keep it in my mind and life. John 14:6 teaches us that Jesus is the way to the Father, and no one comes to the Father any other way.

Keep in mind that Jesus is the Word of God. "In the beginning was the Word, and the Word was with God, and the Word was God. And the Word was made flesh, and dwelt among us, (and we beheld His glory, the glory as the only begotten of the Father,) full of grace and truth" (John 1:1,14). Revelation 19:13 says, "and His name is called The Word of God."

So plainly, the way to get into the presence of God is by the Word of God. This is also the way to get into the very presence of Jesus as the Father, Son, and the Holy Ghost are One (see 1 John 5:5-8).

John 4:24 says that God is a Spirit and we who worship Him must worship Him in spirit and in truth. The word worship is the Hebrew word *proskuneō* that is coequally rendered as: near to. So if you want to get near to Jesus, you must do it by truth—and the highest truth in existence is God's Word. John 17:17 says, "Sanctify them through Thy truth: Thy word is truth."

God's Word allows us to get near to Jesus!

By the Grace of God

We need to understand that God has already given us all things that pertain to life and God-likeness (see 2 Pet. 1:3-4). If you read my book *Mystery of the Ages,* you will find over 700 other verses just in the New Testament saying the same thing as Second Peter 1:3-4—only using different words.

So it is a divine privilege of privileges for Jesus to appear to a person. However, we must understand it is not based upon religious deeds or our goodness that He appears. This privilege has been paid for by the blood of Jesus (see Rom. 8:32). At the same time, there is a pathway to the presence of Jesus, and it is the Word of God. John 14:6 says, "Jesus saith unto him, I am the way, the truth, and the life: no man cometh unto the Father, but by Me." The Word, which is the highest order of truth, is the *way.*

As you study the life of the Saul, before he became the apostle Paul, you find that he went to the best Bible schools of his day. So he knew the Word of God very well—and Jesus appeared to him. Acts 9:3-5 says, "And as he journeyed, he came near Damascus: and suddenly there shined round about him a light from heaven: And he fell to the earth, and heard a voice saying unto him, Saul, Saul, why persecutest thou Me? And he said, Who are Thou, Lord? And the Lord said, I am Jesus…."

Even though Saul (who became Paul) was a very evil man who was persecuting believers, Jesus appeared to him; because, I believe, Saul knew the Word of God.

Before he accepted Jesus as his Lord, he went around destroying, slaughtering, and murdering families simply because they believed in Jesus. Acts 8:3 says, "As for Saul, he made havoc of the church, entering into every house, and haling men and women committed them to prison." The Greek word for havoc is *lumainomai,* which can be expressed as: to destroy, shattering into minute fragments, lacerate.

So it is obvious that Jesus did not appear to Saul based on his goodness or even because he was a Christian—because he was neither.

Acts 9:1 says, "And Saul, yet breathing out threatenings *and slaughter* against the disciples of the Lord, went unto the high priest." The phrase "and slaughter" is one word in the Greek, *phonos,* which means: murder, to slay.

You may be reading this book thinking that you have to earn some kind of religious lifestyle in order for Jesus to appear to you, as if Jesus only appears to special people. Well, every human being is just as valuable and precious to Jesus as the next—and He wants to appear to every person. However, the pathway to Jesus appearing to you is knowing the Word of God.

Love Fulfills All of God's Word

Let's look at some verses that show that if we allow God's unconditional love to rule in our lives, this allows all of God's Word to be fulfilled in our lives. And this puts us in a position for Jesus to appear to us.

If you love one another unconditionally, you fulfill John 14:21.

The Bible says in Romans 13:8 to "love one another: for he that loveth another hath fulfilled the law." The Greek word for law is *nomos,* which means: specifically (of Moses); also of the Gospel. Clearly by loving other people, we fulfill all of God's purpose, all of His will, all of His Word.

Love is the fulfilling of the law. The word law is the same word used in Romans 13:8. Clearly God's unconditional love that rules in our lives fulfills John 14:21. So as a person allows unconditional Love to rule in his or her life, this opens the door to having a personal manifestation of Jesus appear to the person.

Matthew 22:37-40 says, "Jesus said unto him, Thou shalt love the Lord thy God with all the heart, and with all thy soul, and with all thy mind. This is the first and great commandment. And the second is like unto it, Thou shalt love thy neighbor as thyself. On these two commandments hang all the law and the prophets." Again the word law is the same exact Greek word, *nomos,* as in Romans 13:8; which is in reference to all of the Old Testament and New Testament.

So again we see another passage that validates this concept of allowing God's unconditional love to rule in our lives, so that we then fulfill all of God's Word in our lives, which also fulfills John 14:21.

First John 4:7-9 says, "Beloved, let us love one another: for love is of God; and every one that loveth is born of God, and knoweth God. He that loveth not knoweth not God; for God is love. *In this was manifested* the love of God toward us...." The word manifested is the Greek word *phaneroō.* This word is rendered as: appear, shew self.

When we love one another: Number 1, we are born of God. This causes us to become one of God's supernatural children. Number 2, this unconditional love ruling in us is another reason why we have manifestations of Jesus appearing and showing Himself to us.

Ephesians 3:19 also gives us clear teaching concerning God's unconditional love ruling in our lives as a foundation for Jesus appearing to us. "And to know the love of Christ, which passeth knowledge, that ye might be filled with all the fullness of God." The phrase, "And to know" is one Greek word, *ginōskō,* which is rendered as: allow, feel, speak.

When you speak words of unconditional love toward others, when you allow God's unconditional love to rule in your thought life and actions, when you cause your hands to reach out and touch people with God's unconditional love to purposely, gently touch people in a godly way, by doing these actions of God's unconditional love, you are truly knowing God's unconditional love and it causes you to be filled with the fullness of God. If you are filled with God's fullness, it is a simple thing to have Jesus appear to you.

Being Spiritually-Minded

Romans 8:6 says, "For to be carnally minded is death; but to be spiritually-minded is life and peace." The Greek word for life is *zoe.* This word is coequally rendered as life the way God has it. In John 6:63, Jesus said, "It is the spirit that quickeneth; the flesh profiteth nothing: the words that I speak unto you, they are spirit, and they are life." God's Word is *Spirit!*

So by reading these two verses, it is plain that the more of God's Word that people have in them, the more spiritually-minded they will be; and the more spiritually-minded they are, the more God's will registers in their lives. If we have life the way God has it, we will see Jesus as He lives in divine life.

Looking at Enoch

In Genesis 5:24, the Bible says, "And Enoch walked with God: and he was not; for God took him." The Hebrew word for walked in this verse is *hâlak,* which means: be conversant, follow, travel, to and fro, up and down, to places, wander, [way-] faring man.

John 4:24 teaches us plainly, "God is a Spirit: and they that worship Him *must* worship Him in spirit and in truth." The Greek word for worship is *proskuneo* which expresses: to be near to Him in spirit and in truth. And Jesus said in John 6:63 that His words are spirit. And then He said in John 17:17 that His word is truth.

Let's put these facts together: Enoch walked with and was very near to God, he conversed and traveled with God. If God went up or down, Enoch went with Him. The only way Enoch could have possibly done this is because he was near to God by the Word of God in his spirit, mind, and life; they who are near God *must* do it only one way, by Spirit and Truth, which is the Word.

I believe and have already established that the way to get into God's presence is by the Word of God; and the more of God's Word you have in your life, the more you will have divine life. So it is very clear that Enoch must have had a lot of God's Word in his life by the description of the word *walked*. It appears that Enoch constantly conversed with God, followed God, and every place Enoch went he was aware of God's presence.

Keep in mind that we have a New Covenant established upon better promises; if Enoch could have this kind of experience of seeing God, how much more can we as people of the Better Covenant, the New Covenant. Notice the following Scripture confirmations: "For the law made nothing perfect, but the bringing in of that better hope did...Jesus made a surety of a better testament" (Heb. 7:19, 22). "But now hath He obtained a more excellent ministry, by how much also He is the mediator of a better covenant, which was established upon better promises" (Heb. 8:6).

I believe these passages establish the fact that by having God's Word as a high priority in a person's life, the door is opened into the very presence of the Lord.

Enoch conversed with God so much that he discovered how to walk into Heaven; and then one day he simply decided to stay in Heaven. As you study the Scriptures, you may realize that this type of experience is not supposed to happen until the millennial reign of Jesus on the earth. So in my opinion, this validates that people can actually jump dispensations when God's Word is first place in their lives.

Enoch saw God because of the Word of God in his mind, spirit, and life!

Looking at Ezekiel

*Now it came to pass in the thirtieth year, in the fourth month, in the fifth day of the month, as I was among the captives by the river of Chebar, that the heavens were opened, and **I saw visions of God**. In the fifth day of the month, which was the fifth year of king Jehoiachin's captivity,* ***the word of the Lord came*** *expressly unto Ezekiel the priest, the son of Buzi, in the land of the Chaldeans by the river Chebar; and the hand of the Lord was there upon him* (Ezekiel 1:1-3).

The Hebrew word came in verse 3 is *hâyâh,* which means: committed, continue, require. By looking at what is being said in these verses and then with the fuller understanding of the word, came, I believe that because God's Word was *continually a requirement* in Ezekiel's life, *he saw visions of God!*

Keep in mind that we have a new covenant established upon better promises, whatever God did for people of the Old Testament, He will do for us and more (see Heb. 7:22; 8:6).

God's Word needs to be a requirement in our lives just like water is a requirement. When we really understand what God's Word does for us, it is not bondage at all; just like it is not bondage to drink water. We read and study it because of the fulfillment that comes into our lives. And then it causes our spirits to be sensitive to the spirit world where Jesus lives; and He lives right next to us, as He said He will never leave us nor forsake us (see Heb. 13:5). If

Jesus will never leave us nor forsake us, surely we ought to be able to see Him sometime.

Looking at Leviticus

*Also a bullock and a ram for peace offerings, to sacrifice before the Lord; and a meat offering mingled with oil: for today **the Lord will appear unto you!** And Moses said, This is the thing which the Lord commanded that ye should do: and **the glory of the Lord shall appear** unto you. ...and the glory of the **Lord appeared unto all the people**. ...when all **the people saw,** they shouted, and fell on their faces* (Leviticus 9:4,6,23-24).

In the Old Testament, God had conditions in order for Him to appear to people. The conditions were sacrifice offerings. *In the New Testament, Jesus offered Himself as the greatest sacrificial offering* that could be ever offered to God. So how much more do we today have the right for Jesus to appear to us!

Being in the Spirit

Another way we can say we are keeping and loving God's commandments is the phrase, "being in the Spirit." Keep in mind the Spirit of God is the Word of God (see John 6:63).

So if a person is really in the Spirit or walking or living in the Spirit they are walking and living in the Word of God.

Look at John's experience while he was on the isle of Patmos. He was in the Spirit on the Lord's day and He saw Jesus. Revelation 1:10-13 says, "I was in the Spirit on the Lord's day, and heard behind me a great voice, as of a trumpet, saying, I am Alpha and Omega, the first and the last... And I turned to see the voice that spake with me. And being turned, I saw...one like unto the Son of man."

Revelation 4:2,5 says, "And immediately I was in the spirit; and, behold, a throne was set in heaven, and One sat on the throne. And out of the throne proceeded lightnings and thunderings and voices: and there were seven lamps of fire burning before the throne, which are the seven Spirits of God."

John was allowing God's Word to rule and live in his mind, spirit, and life; and that was the channel or the way that allowed Jesus to appear to him in a marvelous, supernatural way. This experience was extremely life-changing for John, and it gave us the wonderful, powerful Book of Revelation.

The appearance of Jesus will do the same for us today.

Jesus Is Always With Us

For where two or three are gathered together in my name, there am I in the midst of them (Matthew 18:20).

Jesus was not saying that it takes two or three to be gathered in His name for Him to be there; He was saying wherever His Word is, He will be there—as He is the Word of God.

Another point is that Jesus is the Word of God (see John 1:1,14; Rev. 19:13). So wherever the Word of God is, Jesus is there. So if He is there, I believe that we should be able to see Him sometimes.

Hebrews 13:5 says, "for He hath said, 'I will never leave thee, nor forsake thee.'"

DNA

I am convinced that some people are born more spiritually-minded than others. By observation and reading about different people groups, it appears that some people groups are more spiritually-minded.

For example, the Bible is the greatest source of information about God in all of existence. The Bible's content is comprised predominately of stories and the history of Jewish people written by Jewish authors. Therefore, I believe the Jewish people are the most spiritually-minded people in the world. In the Bible, they were consistently seeing and experiencing the supernatural, spiritual world. They were seeing angels, having Jesus appear to them, having visions, hearing supernatural, spiritual audible voices, and doing supernatural feats.

By my travels in many countries and dealing with many people types, I find that American Indians are also one of the more spiritually-minded groups. By my studies and observation, I think there is a strong possibility that American Indians are one of the lost tribes of Israel. I have a book that was written in 1825 and published by an American archaeological company in the United States that presents information that all of the American Indian tribes use Hebrew words in their languages. Also, much of their lifestyles and governmental structure are exactly the same. Both people groups have similar governmental outlines, such as tribes, warriors, arrows, shields, and the list goes on.

Pastor Moore, an Indian friend of mine, was invited to various banquets and ceremonies held by a president of the United States. He told me that he was close to a well-known scientist and was told by him that American Indians use part of their brain that many people groups do not use; and this part of the brain causes them to be more spiritually-minded.

Through study, I found that all people have been created with the same type of brains. However, some people use part of their brains to sing proficiently, while others use their brains for mathematical equations. In some people groups there are stronger traits than in others. This does not mean that one person or people group is better than another, just that different parts of the brain are used in different ways.

I would also like to say, just because a person is not in a people group that has a certain God-given talent, it is no reason that he or she cannot learn to be very proficient with that talent.

For example, not all people are born with the DNA to sing; but all people can learn to sing. However, the person who is born with the natural ability to sing has a much easier road to success. I've known people who were not born to sing. For many years it was difficult for them to sing on-key and to have much of a quality of voice for singing. However, because of much, much effort, they learned to be some of the best singers in the United States at a very early age in life.

In like manner, all people can learn to be spiritually-minded and have visions and spiritual encounters.

Over the years, Jesus has appeared to me a few times. I have written down some of these times, as they were extremely important to me, and I did not want to forget the experience or forget what I learned. However, I know that the Lord has appeared to me at other times, and unless the Lord brings these times and experiences to my remembrance, they will remain forgotten to me.

I share with you only what He brought to my remembrance. When I started writing this book, the Lord woke me up and brought to my remembrance a couple of other times that I did not write down, so I share these also.

I will tell you about the nine times Jesus appeared to me—that I do remember and that the Lord is instructing me to share—and provide Scriptures to support what Jesus taught me.

Faith Comes From Hearing

I've preached in more churches than I could possibly remember throughout the world; and by observation, I've found that churches that have not been taught about being born again have no born-again members. Likewise, churches that do not teach healing, miracles, or prosperity—no one in those churches receive those blessings.

The Bible teaches us in Romans 10:17 that *faith comes by hearing and hearing* by the Word of God. The word faith in this passage is the Greek word *pistis*. This Greek word means: especially reliance upon Christ for salvation, assurance, belief, believe. The root or foundational word for this Greek word is *peitho* meaning: truth, evidence of authority, confidence, trust. The phrase, "cometh by hearing" and the phrase "and hearing" is one Greek word, *akoe* meaning: the act, the sense or the thing heard: audience, report.

Clearly as we hear by the preaching or teaching of God's Word or by giving audience to God's Word by reading it, this gives us faith, assurance, authority, confidence, and trust in God's Word for that particular blessing!

You can see this truth throughout the Word of God. Look at Acts 14:8-10, "And there sat a certain man at Lystra, impotent in his feet, being a cripple from his mother's womb, who never had walked: The same heard Paul speak: who steadfastly beholding him, and perceiving that he had faith to be healed, Said with a loud voice, Stand upright on thy feet. And he leaped and walked."

Notice that the man was crippled from birth, then he *heard* the Word of God being taught by Apostle Paul. The crippled man received faith by hearing and then received his miracle!

There are many, many examples of this truth throughout the Word of God. As you read the Word, look for these truths.

People who have never heard or read about healing, miracles, prosperity, and salvation do not receive these blessings. However, after they read or hear about the goodness and mercies of God, their faith is built up and they receive these miracles.

In like manner, by reading this book, you will build up your faith to have Jesus appear to you!

CHAPTER 2

Four Different Kinds of Visions

In this chapter I present Scriptures revealing four different kinds of visions. There are four different ways that Jesus appears to people today: *chazon, chizzayon, marah,* and *erchomaier.* I will explain each, including the Hebrew words.

1. Chazon (pronounced Khawzone)

I call this type of a vision, a mental vision. Proverbs 29:18 reads, "Where there is no *vision,* the people perish: but he that keepeth the *law,* happy is he."

The Hebrew word for vision in Proverbs 29:18 is *chazon* and means: a sight (mentally), dream, a revelation or oracle. The root word for this word means: mentally to *perceive, contemplate* (with pleasure); specifically to *have a vision of: provide.*

The word, "law" in this passage is the Hebrew word *torah,* which means statute, Pentateuch, especially the Decalogue.

Note that the word, *Pentateuch* refers to the first five books of the Bible. And the word *Decalogue* references the Ten Commandments with the intent of leading people to Jesus and His teachings.

As you read this passage in Proverbs, notice that the word vision and the word law are rendered as coequal terms in this passage; even though they are different Hebrew words.

Every language does this. For example, you can be talking about a man and refer to him throughout your discourse as a: male, husband, father, and the list can go on; however, all of these words, even though they are different words, are all referring to the man.

In God's Word, in Proverbs 29:18, I believe that God is saying that if you keep the law—the Word of God—you will be happy, because you will have revelations and oracles that you have initiated with your mental faculties.

It is my opinion that we can read Proverbs 29:18 this way and be accurate scripturally: People who read God's Word can purposely have mental pictures based on God's Word, and they are happy people.

These kind of people have a fulfillment in their lives that is divinely supernatural.

Every Christian should have mental visions, mentally seeing God's Word as truth.

For example, Hebrews 13:5 plainly teaches us that Jesus will never leave us nor forsake us. So we should constantly initiate mental visions of Jesus being at our side. Doing this gives us incredible spiritual strength, happiness, and fulfillment in life.

As you study the Scriptures, you will find God's heroes were people who purposely had mental visions.

Look at Acts 2:25, "For David speaketh concerning Him, I foresaw the Lord always before my face, for He is on my right hand, that I should not be moved." Also, Matthew 5:8, "Blessed are the pure in heart: for they shall see God."

There is a lot of great teaching concerning this subject; however at this time, I do not want to spend much time with just this thought, as this is not my major discourse.

I do want to say that this type of vision is extremely important. All of the experiences that I mention in this book are not in reference to this type of vision at all. This type of vision is self-initiated; the visions I've had of the Lord Jesus that I mention later in this book were God-initiated.

This type of vision is the simplest, and any one can have these kinds of visions anytime they want—based on the Word of God that they know, as it is seeing God's Word as truth.

This type of vision is really the most important; as it plainly says in Proverbs 29:18 that if we do not have these types of visions, we will perish.

This type of vision is the simplest and is purposely self-initiated. I highly recommend all Christians to purposely have visions like this every day. This type of vision causes a person to be more spiritually-minded and in turn opens a person up to more of God's spiritual world of visions, His supernatural gifts.

Notice that Romans 8:5-6 says, "For they that are after the flesh do mind things of the flesh; but they that are after the Spirit things of the Spirit. For to be carnally minded is death: but to be *spiritually minded is life.*" The Greek word for life in this passage is *zoe,* which is coequally rendered as: life the way God has it, and peace.

Philippians 2:5 states, "*Let* this ["let this" is the Greek word *touto,* which means accusative] mind be in you, which was in Christ Jesus...."

In just these two verses (and there are many, many more that a book could be written) the decision is ours: *We must choose* to be spiritually-minded. We must let, cause, this mind that was in Christ, to be in us.

2. Chizzayon

I call the second type of vision a dream vision. *Chizzayon* is a Hebrew word meaning a revelation, especially by dream—vision.

This word is used in Job 33:15, "In a dream, in a vision of the night, when deep sleep falleth upon men, in slumberings upon the bed." Many dreams are visions; ordained of God, they are actually spiritual encounters.

The purpose of this chapter is to influence you to have great confidence in God-ordained dreams, because they are visions initiated by God; visions of God. You will also learn how to know if it is a God-ordained dream (vision from God).

Out of the nine times that Jesus appeared to me, seven times I saw Him in a dream while my natural body was sleeping. One time was in the flesh when I was totally awake, and I saw and felt Jesus the same way I would see and feel any natural human being. One time I saw Him while I was wide awake, and He was in a spiritual manifestation. I could see through Him, but at the same time I could see Him well enough that I could see every feature about Him.

Looking at Dreams

Looking at God's Word you can see that some dreams are clearly visions ordained of God. During the night session while a person is in bed in deep sleep and slumberings, this is a time of having dreams; see Job 33:14-15. However in this passage from Job, God calls this experience a vision.

You will also notice that God highly endorses these experiences. God says that this is a time when He speaks to people and seals their instructions. God wants to give us God-ordained instructions in our dreams.

I want to also point out that this passage mentions that God speaks once and twice during the day session; however, many times we are so physically and mentally busy that we do not perceive or hear God's voice during the day session. So God waits until our bodies and our minds cannot distract or interfere with Him communicating with us. God loves us so much and wants to bless us so much, that He will do what He has to do to get our attention. When our bodies are in deep sleep and our minds are shut down, He will then try to communicate to us in a dream—a vision of the night.

Let's again read Job 33:14-16, "For God speaketh once, yea twice, yet man perceiveth it not. In a dream, in *a vision of the night,* when deep sleep falleth upon men, in slumberings upon the bed; Then He openeth the ears of men, and sealeth their instruction."

Knowing that God speaks to us through dreams will cause us to take our dreams more seriously. We must pray for God to give us the interpretation of our dreams and search the Scriptures for God's validation.

Dreams Saved Jesus' Life

You will notice by reading the first two chapters of Matthew that Jesus' life was saved because of people having dreams and knowing that God was giving them divine instructions.

Jesus coming to this earth was either the first or second most important thing that God could do for human beings from the beginning of time; and it came to pass because of the confidence of people believing in dreams. This truth lets us know clearly that dreams are either the first or second most important communication we receive from the Lord.

In the New Testament, dreams are extremely ordained ways that God communicated His divine order to people.

Let's look at a few passages that show clearly that Jesus' life was saved because of people having dreams and knowing that dreams were divine communication from God:

Then Joseph her husband, being a just man, and not willing to make her a public example, was minded to put *her away privily. But while he thought on these things, behold, the angel of the Lord appeared unto him **in a dream,** saying, Joseph, thou son of David, fear not to take unto thee Mary thy wife: for that which is conceived in her is of the Holy Ghost. Then Joseph being raised from sleep did as the angel of the Lord had bidden him, and took unto him his wife* (Matthew 1:19-20,24).

Stop and think about this. A young man is dating a young lady. She tells him she is pregnant and says she conceived by the Holy Ghost. It would take an extremely spiritually in-tune with God young man to believe such a story.

This never happened before and has not since. In those days sex before marriage was the death sentence. So Joseph was endangering his life to have anything to do with Mary. *And the convincing tool was a dream.* So Joseph married Mary. (Notice the death sentence for sex outside of marriage in these passages: Deuteronomy 22:21-24; John 8:3-5; Leviticus 20:10-12.)

The Jewish people knew that God gave divine dreams to communicate His greatest concerns for humanity. So if dreams are valid for God's greatest concern for humanity, we can absolutely trust them for our everyday concerns.

*And being warned of God **in a dream** that they should not return to Herod, they departed into their own country another way* (Matthew 2:12).

In the previous verses of Matthew 2, the wise men from the East were coming to Bethlehem of Judea to honor Jesus and give gifts to His parents; knowing that Jesus was the Messiah. However, Herod the king instructed the wise men to let him know where Jesus was. And of course Herod wanted to kill Jesus. But again these wise men received instructions in a *dream* not to return to Herod. They obeyed the dream; and again, Jesus' life was saved because men believed in a dream.

*And when they were departed, behold, the angel of the Lord appeareth to Joseph **in a dream**, saying, Arise, and take the young Child and His mother, and flee into Egypt, and be thou there until I bring thee word: for Herod will seek the young Child to destroy Him. When he arose, he took the young Child and His mother by night, and departed into Egypt: And was there until the death of Herod: that it might be fulfilled which was spoken of the Lord by the prophet, saying, Out of Egypt have I called My Son* (Matthew 2:13-15).

Here again, Jesus' life was saved, and the course of Joseph and Mary's life was changed because of their confidence in a dream.

*But when Herod was dead, behold, an angel of **the Lord appeareth in a dream** to Joseph in Egypt, saying, Arise, and take the young Child and His mother, and go into the land of Israel: for they are dead which sought the young Child's life. And he arose, and took the young Child and His mother, and came into the land of Israel* (Matthew 2:19-21).

Joseph once again had a dream, and had confidence that it was God giving him divine instructions to save the life of Jesus and change the course of his life and Mary's.

If people today would realize that God still gives divine instructions with dreams, lives would be saved, they could experience greater things in life, and they would have God's blessings upon their lives.

I've known of people who have had dreams and they discredited the dreams as nightmares. Instead of getting out of bed and praying until they received God's interpretation, they dismissed the dream. Then a few days went by and the nightmare turned into a natural disaster that could have been totally avoided—if they would have realized it was God warning them and heeded His warning.

> *But when he heard that Archelaus did reign in Judaea in the room of his father Herod, he was afraid to go thither: notwithstanding,* ***being warned of God in a dream,*** *he turned aside into the parts of Galilee: And he came and dwelt in a city called Nazareth: that it might be fulfilled which was spoken by the prophets, He shall be called a Nazarene* (Matthew 2:22-23).

Today we have the same God, and He is giving dreams so the Word of God and prophecies from the Word of God, from the heart of God, can be fulfilled. When we have dreams, we need to pray and find Scriptures (at least three clear verses by different authors in the Bible: see Matt. 18:16; 2 Cor. 13:1) that interpret our dreams. And then we need to make plans and take actions to make the dream come to pass in this natural world—or heed the warning in the dream and make plans so the dream of warning does not come to pass.

Also know that not all dreams are of God. However, if we seek the Lord and find Scripture to support the instructions or warnings of the dream, we can then determine if it is a God-given dream or not.

We must understand that dreams are actual spiritual encounters. Dreams are of the realm where God lives, and God-given dreams are more real than the natural world. A God-given dream is an experience in the dimension of God.

*When he was set down on the judgment seat, his wife sent unto him, saying, Have thou nothing to do with that just Man: for **I have suffered many things this day in a dream** because of Him* (Matthew 27:19).

Here we find the story of Pilate's wife being warned of God in a dream. She did not want Pilate to do anything wrong against Jesus. Pilate and his wife actually suffered because Pilate did not fully heed the warning of a dream. However, Pilate's wife knew that she had a divine encounter to warn her husband.

Hebrew and Greek Words

The Hebrew word *chazon* is found 34 times in the Old Testament and it means dream or vision, in the Hebrew.

The Hebrew word *chizzâyôn* is used in the Old Testament nine times, and also means dream or vision.

The Hebrew word *chêzev* is found in the Old Testament 12 times and its root word is *chazon*.

The Greek word *optanomai* is used 56 times in the New Testament, and it means appear, look, see, shew self, to *gaze* (that is, with wide open eyes, as at something remarkable). Most of the time this word is rendered as: to see or appear. However, it is rendered many times as seeing God or Jesus as a Spirit or them appearing.

Note: even though this word is not rendered as a dream or a vision, it is used when a person has a dream or a vision in the New Testament, and has the same basic meaning as a dream or a vision.

The Greek word *hora* is the root word for *optanomai* and is translated as vision or an inspired appearance. Note again that this word is not rendered as a dream but has the same meaning as in the Scriptures where dreams ordained of God are inspired appearances.

The Greek word *horasis* is found three times in the New Testament and is rendered as vision or the act of *gazing*, that is, (internal) an inspired *appearance*. Again a different word, but having the same basic meaning of a God-ordained dream.

The Greek word *horama* is used 13 times in the New Testament and means *something gazed at*, that is, a *spectacle* (especially supernatural)—sight, vision. This is another word that clearly defines the word dream but is not translated as a dream when it is used in the New Testament.

The Greek word *optasia* is used three times in the New Testament and is rendered as: *visuality*, that is, (concretely) an *apparition*—vision. Again a brief meaning for the word dream.

The Greek word *enupnion* is used one time in the New Testament and is coequally rendered in the Greek as: something seen *in sleep*, that is, (*vision* in a dream).

3. Marah

I call this type of vision *a spiritual vision*. Marah is a Hebrew word rendered as: a vision, looking glass.

When this type of vision is in manifestation, a person will see an immaterial appearance of an entity or being. If you were to see Jesus with this type of vision, you would see the details of Him, but He would be transparent. He would be more spiritual.

Daniel 10:7 gives us an excellent example, "And I Daniel alone saw the vision: for the men that were with me saw not the vision; but a great quaking fell upon them, so that they fled to hide themselves."

4. Erchomaier

I call this type of vision *a physical vision*. The Greek word *erchomaier* is used in John 20:26-28. It reads:

And after eight days again His disciples were within, and Thomas with them: then came Jesus, the doors being shut, and stood in the midst, and said, Peace be unto you. Then saith He to Thomas, Reach hither thy finger, and behold My hands; and reach hither thy hand, and thrust it into My side: and be not faithless, but believing. And Thomas answered and said unto Him, my Lord and my God.

Note that the phrase in verse 26, "with them: then came" is the Greek word, *erchomaier* and it is translated as: accompany, appear, light.

In this type of vision, Jesus would be as physical as any other normal human being. But He would also be so spiritual that He could walk through a wall, as He did in the case with the disciples in John 20:26. There are times when Jesus appears like this and is in the form of a servant, as spelled out in Philippians 2:7 and Mark 16:12.

CHAPTER 3

The Dispensation of Visions

In this chapter I establish the fact that we are in the same dispensation as the people in the New Testament. Therefore, everything of the New Testament belongs to us today (see Heb. 7:22; 8:6; Matt. 11:11). Everything that God did for any person in the New Testament He will do for us as well.

We will be looking through the New Testament, which reveals quite a few instances when Jesus appeared to people after He died.

The first two people Jesus appeared to were Mary Magdalene and the mother of James.

Keep in mind that Mary Magdalene was a prostitute before she met Jesus. However, God forgives and forgets our past! Jesus appearing to people is not based upon how wonderful we are; it is based upon how wonderful God is. Again you see the grace and mercy of God in Acts 9:1-6 when Jesus appeared to Saul while he was in a strong, sinful state.

Stop and think; if God appears to a person who was slaughtering disciples of Jesus and a person with a sinful past, then I believe He wants to and will appear to anyone.

After Jesus appeared to Mary Magdalene and Mary the mother of James, He then appeared to two of His followers, then the eleven disciples (see Mark 16).

Jesus also appeared to Cephas, then 500 at one time. Then James and Apostle Paul (see 1 Cor. 15:4-8).

In Second Corinthians 12:7, Paul makes the statement that he had an *"abundance of the revelations."* The phrase "abundance of the revelations" is the Greek word *apokalupsis,* which in the Greek, and different places in the Scripture, means appearing. And we know that Paul had an abundance of times of Jesus appearing to him, as he just mentioned that he was caught up to the third Heaven and, of course, he would have seen Jesus there.

This statement correlates with Paul's statement in Galatians 1:11-12, "But I certify you, brethren, the gospel which was preached of me is not after man. For I neither received it of man, neither was I taught it, but *by the revelation of Jesus Christ."* The phrase, "it, but by the revelation" is also the Greek word *apokalupsis.*

To validate that Jesus appeared to Apostle Paul an abundance of times teaching him the Word of God, let's examine Galatians 2:1-2, "Then fourteen years after I went up again to Jerusalem with Barnabas, and took Titus with me also. And I went *up by revelation,* and communicated unto them that gospel which I preach among the Gentiles, but privately to them which were of reputation, lest by any means I should run, or had run, in vain." The phrase " up by revelation" is also *apokalupsis.*

This strongly validates the word *apokalupsis* being used as appearing, as Paul went with Barnabas and Titus and communicated to the people there. Paul did this by physically appearing to them.

I believe this confirms that we can expect the same privileges as we are in the same dispensation. We can expect Jesus to appear to us as we are New Testament people also!

God is no respecter of persons (see Acts 10:34; Rom. 2:11). For God respects all persons the same.

Today we hear testimonies as never before of Jesus appearing to people. This is the will of God to enhance people's lives, and I strongly encourage you to stay open to Jesus appearing to you.

Again, I encourage you to analyze every vision or spiritual appearance with God's Word.

Be encouraged to know that what God will do for one, He will do for all.

CHAPTER 4

God's Unconditional Love
in the Last Days

The vision of Jesus explored in this chapter has put a foundation of God's unconditional love in my life that no human words can fully explain. *Divinely supernatural* are the best words I know in trying to explain the awsomeness of this vision. While my wife, Donna, and I and our oldest daughter, Cherish, were pastoring a church in Taylor, Texas, I went to bed on the Tuesday evening of November 14, 1978. At some point after going to sleep, I was awakened by an angelic or divine person in my bedroom. This being reached down his right hand to take my left hand. For some reason, I did not see a face, as if I was not supposed to see a face. All I saw was this being that appeared to be about six feet tall wearing a brighter-than-the-noonday-sun robe and taking me by the left hand—we immediately went straight up through the roof. As I was going up, I looked back and saw my physical body lying asleep next to Donna. It seemed to be only a second or two, and then I was in Heaven; and my escort was gone.

I was now in a very large banquet room. It seemed to be as large as a city. I saw only a few people standing around. I noticed the tables were gorgeously set with plates, silverware and sparkling goblets; but no food. I knew this was the preparation of the marriage supper of the Lamb, which is to take place immediately after the Rapture.

Back when I had this experience, I thought the Rapture was going to take place very soon. However, Second Peter 3:8 says, "But beloved, be not ignorant, be not ignorant of this one thing, that one day is with the Lord as a thousand years, and a thousand years as one day."

I noticed at a distance of about 30 feet directly in front of me, my grandfather was standing. Arnie Bray, my grandfather, had passed away May 9, 1975. I noticed that he had a very angelic body. My grandfather was about 5 feet 10 inches and was in bad health and only weighed about 130 pounds when he died. But now as I looked at him, he had a healthy, athletic body. He wore a gray worker's suit with long sleeves, so I could not see the definition of his arms. But it was obvious that he had large arms with biceps of about 25 inches. His whole body matched his arms; he was extremely powerful looking and seemed to be about 40 years of age. When he passed away, he was 71.

I ran to him and said, "Grandpa, it is so good to see you!" I embraced him. Normally my grandfather would have been very affectionate; however, I noticed that his hug toward me was not as loving as I expected. I backed up a little, and he reached both of his arms out and took hold of my arms and looked me in the eyes with great concern. There was love in his eyes but a greater concern of urgency. He said to me, "You have to go back and warn everyone to walk in love." And then he said, "Many are not going to make it because they do not walk in love."

If you ever see an angel, Jesus, or someone in Heaven, you will notice that they do not have to say much, yet it means a great deal. Sometimes they may not speak; but information is transmitted into your spirit and mind in great volumes. So I knew what my grandfather was saying—many people who profess to be Christians will not be included in the Rapture because they do not let unconditional love (which is God, see First John 4:7-8) rule in their lives.

What my grandfather told me still pierces my heart today. He was saying that he knew by the knowledge that God permeates throughout Heaven that many people who go to church all of the time and do a lot of religious things such as church traditions, were not going to Heaven if they did not let God's unconditional love be the foundation of their person.

It reminded me of the passage in Matthew 7:21-23:

Not everyone that saith unto Me, Lord, Lord, shall enter into the kingdom of heaven; but he that doeth the will of My Father which is in heaven. Many will say to Me in that day, Lord, Lord, have we not prophesied in Thy name? And in Thy name have cast out devils? And in Thy name done many wonderful works? And then will I profess unto them, I never knew you: depart from Me, ye that work iniquity.

At that time in my life, I had been pastoring churches and doing crusades for about six years, and I had a tendency to preach a lot of condemnation. Jude 4 says, "For there are certain men crept in unawares, who were before of old ordained to this condemnation, ungodly men...."

Note that condemnation is an ordination, not for godly men and women, but for ungodly men and women.

The beginning of anything is its foundation. And the foundation of anything is the most important part of that thing. This is true with the Christian life; immediately after a person is born again he or she is instantly ordained into the ministry of reconciliation. Second Corinthians 5:17 says, "Therefore if any *man* (man is the Greek word *ei tis i tis* and means whosoever) be in Christ, *he is* ("he is" means vitalized in most Bibles, indicating these words are not at all in the Greek Bibles. You will find this to be true as you look these words up in a Greek or Hebrew concordance) a new creature: old things are passed away; behold all things are become new."

Notice that in the very next verse we are given the ministry of reconciliation by God. Then in the next verse, God talks about the ministry that He has given us and says, "He committed unto us the word of reconciliation" (2 Cor. 5:19). The word committed in this passage is the Greek word *tithemi,* which is rendered as ordain. So immediately after we are born again, we are ordained by God into the ministry of reconciliation.

Since we are here, let's examine the ministry of reconciliation that we are ordained into by God.

The word reconciliation is the Greek word *katallag ,* which means restoration to (the divine) favor, exchange.

So immediately after we are born again, we are in the ministry of telling the world that God is not condemning them, but He is offering them divine favor to be greatly blessed in this life and have eternal life in Heaven. So I believe that the foundation of all ministries and all Christians is reconciliation.

Since November 14, 1978, when I was translated to Heaven, I've notice there is a special inspiration in my spirit and mind as I read the Word of God *to always look for the love of God in every Scripture passage.* If we do not read unconditional love in any passage in the Holy Scriptures, we are reading it incorrectly. For God is unconditional love, and He is the same yesterday, today, and forever (see 1 John 4:7-8,16; Heb. 13:8).

He Is Coming for a Glorious People

One evening in the fall of 1984, I went to sleep and woke up standing in Heaven. I saw Jesus, and He asked me to come with Him as He wanted to show me something. He took me to the most beautiful flower garden I have ever seen. I really do not know for sure how large it was, but as far as I could see in every direction there was this garden. In the middle of the garden, in front of Jesus and me, was my grandfather standing on a large ladder making a large wreath. The wreath was made out of beautiful red roses, and the wreath seemed to be about 14-16 feet high. It was the most beautiful thing in the garden.

The wreath was heart shaped, but was not completed yet. The right side still needed to have the hump of the heart filled with roses. I asked Jesus what this wreath in the shape of a heart was for. Jesus told me that the wreath represents the greatest move of God that has ever come upon the earth. This move would be the last move of God on the earth.

That is all that Jesus said, but I knew what He meant. The foundation of the last days'— great signs and wonders that will bring the greatest harvest of souls into the Kingdom of God—will be of God's love. And the people involved with this last days' ministry outpouring will be a people whose foundation and lives are ruled by God's unconditional, agape love.

After having these experiences in 1978 and then in 1984, I have come to understand all of God's Word with unconditional love. If I do not understand a verse anywhere in the Bible without God's unconditional love coming from it, I am simply understanding it incorrectly.

The Hebrew and Greek languages of the Bible bring to light God's unconditional love with verses that do not appear that way. God's unconditional love fulfills every verse in the Bible (see Rom. 13:8,10).

Matthew 22:37-40 says to love the Lord thy God with all of your heart, all of your mind; and love your neighbor after you have learned to love yourself, and then love them as you love yourself. On these two commandments are the foundation of the whole Bible!

I would strongly advise buying the book, *Love the Way to*

Victory by Kenneth Hagin Sr. Brother Hagin wrote some great books. His inspired books of Bible subjects have changed the course of this world by people taking action after reading them. However, I believe that *Love the Way to Victory* is possibly one of his best books. If you follow the biblical truths in his book, as well as the book you are holding, I promise you those truths will take you to a promotion in God that very few Christians have ever experienced.

CHAPTER 5

Understanding Warfare

I learned from the visitation of Jesus I am about to share with you that behind every problem there is a demon; and if we get rid of the demon, we in turn get rid of the problem.

One night in October 1973, I went to sleep, and sometime during the night session I saw Jesus—I assume this was a dream vision. However, it was just as real, in fact more real than any natural happening. Jesus said to me, "Mel, I want to show you something." With His left hand, He took my right hand and we began to walk into a large corridor of a cave. It seemed to be about half a mile wide and I could not see the end. The cave was full of demons that were hideous to look at; and they were making horrible, frightening noises.

The sight alone of just one of these demons was so frightening, so extremely horrifying, that within moments a person with no resisting power would die a horrible death from fright. Just the sounds from one of these demons were more horrifying than the sight of them. For a human to listen to just one of these creatures for more than 30 seconds would frighten them to death.

No human is any match for any demon outside of the power we have in the Lord Jesus. The human mind and body are not equipped for such torment.

To know that hell is full of these demons and their noises and their torment throughout eternity causes me to be filled with an urgency to win as many people to the Lord as I possibly can. All demons are supernatural in the evil sense; and their eternal abode is not meant for any human being. It is totally impossible to ever get to the place where a person is used to the torture. Just these facts alone, of the demonic and supernatural torment that comes from demon-presence in hell, are beyond the comprehension of any human imagination.

And the facts are: there is eternal fire seven times hotter than any heat on the face of the earth along with these demons—and hell is for eternity. The Greek and Hebrew words used for eternal life in Heaven are also used for eternal hell. (Notice the Greek word, "aionios"; it is used 67 times as *everlasting* or *eternal* in the New Testament and seven of those times it is rendered in reference to eternal or everlasting damnation or fire. Look at Matthew 19:16 and 25:41.)

The reality is that no one has to go to hell. God has given every person on earth a free gift of salvation; a free gift to spend eternity in a Heaven of bliss also beyond the human imagination; and it's all free when a person applies Romans 10:9-10 to their life.

After this experience in the demonic cave, I began to

know why people die who overdose on drugs or alcohol. Medical science says they die from an overdose. But when a person cancels out the physical world (which a person does with an overdose), they are then very aware of the spiritual world. They have canceled out the natural, and now they are experiencing the supernatural, demonic world. They are not equipped to handle it, and they are scared to death beyond the human imagination.

Keep in mind, the people who overdose with alcohol, drugs, or any other means that is a demonic influence, give demons the right to take them into deeper realms of the demonic.

While Jesus and I began walking deeper into this corridor, the most horrible, most frightening, most evil demon came running at me swinging his arms and his hands toward my face. His fingers were about 8-10 inches long with fingernails about 4 inches long and curved and extremely sharp. One slash of his fingernails would slice a person in two. As he got closer to me, his arms and hands were swinging toward me with his fingernails slicing through the air, missing my face by fractions of an inch.

Fear came all over me, and then I felt Jesus' left hand grip my right hand. I looked up at Him, as Jesus was about 6 feet tall, and I am 5 feet 10 inches, and He said, "Mel, the rest of your life you will go down corridors just like this, but always remember that I will always be with you." When He finished saying that, all fear vanished, and so did the experience.

That is all that Jesus said; however, in my spirit and mind, Jesus gave me volumes of information. He was telling me that I would have millions and maybe billions of confrontations with all kinds of demons. And to this day, I can say, it would be impossible for me to know how many times since this event I've had confrontations with demon spirits.

There have been more times than I can remember when I was confronted with thousands in one day. I've been to developing countries where satan and demons are reigning supreme. During crusades where there would be as many as 35,000 people in one service, I may have confrontations with 25,000 demons in one service. Keep in mind that every problem that is not of God is of the devil, and there is a demon as the root of that problem.

I wish all people could see and hear in the spirit world as I do; they would then know the truth that we are at war with the devil and his kingdom. I have a free teaching on my Website titled *How to See and Feel in the Spirit*. I provide this so you can learn to operate with the gift of discerning of spirits—a supernatural gift God has given to the whole human race.

Going on with the train of thought of what Jesus fully meant when He talked to me: As I walk in the Spirit, and allow God's unconditional love to rule in my life, I always have more than enough power to resist demons and the devil and cause them to leave.

When Jesus said that He would always be with me, in my spirit and mind Jesus was telling me much more. He was telling me that behind every problem is a demon (see Luke 11:23), and if I take authority over the demon by using Jesus' name, not only would Jesus' presence be there, but also the root of the problem, a demon, would have to leave (see Phil. 2:9). Matthew 18:20 teaches us plainly that wherever Jesus' name is, the Word of God is there, too.

Remembering October 22, 1972

On October 21, 1972, our oldest daughter, Cherish, was born, and Donna was still in the hospital with her. The next morning I was sitting at the breakfast table eating, when all of a sudden I had the most horrible pain in my heart that then went throughout my upper body. The pain was so severe that I knew if I moved it would increase the pain, and I would die. I thought for a moment, and said in my mind, *If I'm going to die, I'm going to die praising the Lord.* So I lifted both of my arms into the air to praise the Lord and instantly all of the pain left.

For about ten years after this experience, I would have chest pains and sometimes it was like electric currents of pain running through the upper part of my body and down one of my arms. I would always pray, and it would go away. The pain was never as bad as it was that morning of October 22.

Then arround 1984, during the night session while I was fast asleep, I had a chest pain in my heart that was much worse than the time back in 1972. It was so excruciating that it instantly woke me up. As soon as I woke up, I saw that same hideous, evil demon that I saw back in October 1973.

He was standing over me grinning with an appearance

that was so horrifying that anyone would die within moments without the safety and power that a child of God has knowing their authority in Christ. This demon's right index finger was in my chest, wrapped around my heart, and his long fingernail was pierced deeply into my heart.

My pain tolerance is fairly high. I've had many things happen to me over the years to cause pain. I could write a fairly good size book telling about the many times I should have died. Like the time a 1,200 pound horse I was riding, for no apparent reason, jumped straight upward and fell backward, landing right on top of me. The only injury was a broken hand.

Another time was when a come-along broke with about 2-3,000 pounds of pressure as I was pulling a very large tree down, cutting it with a chain saw. The chain broke hitting me in the ribs and throwing me at least 6-8 feet backward and into the air—slamming me onto a stump, breaking my ribs in the front and the back. So I know about pain.

However, this pain in my heart caused by the demon was greater than any pain I have ever felt. It was not only natural pain; it was supernatural pain. People who go to hell experience this kind of pain throughout eternity.

As the demon stood over me, I perceived the Lord telling me, "Mel, you do not have a heart problem, it is this demon. If you get rid of the demon, you will get rid of the problem." Keep in mind, when the Lord appears to you, sometimes He does not have to say anything and yet volumes of information are transmitted into your spirit and mind in fractions of a second.

So instantly I said, "I rebuke you in Jesus' name." As I said that not only with my mouth but with godly authority in my spirit, the demon's smile left, and he began to slowly pull his finger out of my chest. I could feel the finger wrapped around my heart loosening. The same degree that the finger was being removed was the same degree of pain leaving my heart and chest. When his finger was finally out of my chest, he vanished; a few minutes later the pain was totally gone.

For the next few years, possibly once a year, there would be an extremely small pain, maybe only one-thirtieth as bad as that night. I knew it was that demon trying to come back to kill me. So I would always speak to it, saying, "In Jesus' name I rebuke you." And the pain would always go. Now it's been at least 25 years with no pain in the least.

Greater is He who is in us than he that is in the world (see 1 John 4:4)!

CHAPTER 6

Guarding Your Mind

This visitation of Jesus caused me to know that what we allow in our minds, what we watch, hinders the supernatural of God from flowing in our lives.

It was the first Tuesday of January 1974; I was in our kitchen in the midst of my morning praying and Bible reading. Nothing exceptional was on my mind. It was just a normal morning. After praying, I walked from the kitchen into the living room doorway. As soon as I was in the doorway, there stood Jesus about 15-20 feet away from me with His right hand on my television. He was looking down toward the television with a serious look of great concern. He was in the form of a Spirit, and I could sort of see through Him, but at the same time, I could see His clothing in detail and His facial features in detail. He was wearing a long robe.

Jesus never moved His mouth, but words came from Him so powerfully. The words were not audible, but they were extremely powerful—supernaturally powerful. I knew if He wanted to direct His Words toward the destruction of the earth that His words had the ability to blow the world into microscopic pieces.

The words that came from Jesus were, "Mel, if you will be cautious what you allow to enter your mind, my gifts will operate in your life in an unprecedented way."

I knew what He meant. Do not let sinful things come into your mind. There are many things on television that no human needs to see. My dad made this statement many years ago, "A lot of what is on TELEVISION is poison!" Sinful thoughts come into our lives one way, by what we look at; and unholy things will stop the holiness of God from being in our lives. Romans 1:4 teaches us plainly that God declared Jesus to be the Son of God with miracle-working power according to the Spirit of holiness. The Greek word for declared in this passage is *horizō,* which means decree, ordain. And the word power in this passage is the Greek word *dunamis,* which means specifically miraculous *power* (usually by implication a *miracle* itself) (worker of) miracle (-s), mighty (wonderful) work. This word is used in the Scriptures in the New Testament as the highest order of God's miracle-working power.

Indeed, Jesus received the highest order of ordination from God because He lived a holy life! He also had the highest order of miracle-working power in His life.

Walking in God's Holiness

If you want this type of holy, miracle-working lifestyle, you must follow His example. And you can, as there are many verses to validate this truth. If you read my book *Mystery of the Ages,* you will see over 700 verses just in the New Testament clearly telling you that God has already given you *all* things that pertain to this life and godliness (God-likeness).

However, sin will blind you. Second Corinthians 4:4 clearly teaches that if you allow sin in your life, it gives satan rights to blind your eyes. Sin has the power to stop the power or the blessings of God, though God is more powerful than sin and the devil. Think about this illustration: Someone gives a person the best car in the world. He learns everything there is to know about the car. He can drive it proficiently. But then he goes blind. He still has the car, he still knows how to drive the car, but if he drives it, he will not go very far without having a wreck and possibly killing himself and others.

After this visitation of Jesus, the very next day, I was in a church service and at least four of the gifts of the Spirit that had never operated in my life previously were in operation with God's great anointing.

What is not good for a child to watch is not good for an adult to watch. Proverbs 23:7 in God's Word says, "For as he [or she] thinketh in his [or her] heart, so is he [or she]."

What we give attention to with our eyes, our bodies, or minds is what we will think about; and that is what we will become. If it is contrary to God, it will blind our eyes from enjoying the wonderful things that the Lord has already given us. Again, God does not withhold from us because of sin in our lives, but sin gives satan rights to blind our eyes so we cannot enjoy God's goodness (see 2 Cor. 4:4).

Chapter 35 of Isaiah is really a book itself. It is a description of what is going to happen in the season before the Rapture. It gives details of great miracles and talks about God's glory (His reputation) being all over the earth.

This chapter also talks about the people who will be involved with this miraculous outpouring of God's glory and power. Verse 8 gives a phrase that is taken from two Hebrew words. That phrase is "it shall be for those: the wayfaring men." Those Hebrew words are *halak* and *derek,* which mean the course of life, because of and by conversation. These people have learned that death and life are in the power of their tongues (see Prov. 18:21). These people who flow in this supernatural power are also coequally living in the way of holiness (also in Isaiah 35:8).

So learning to walk in God's holiness and speaking only things that are in agreement with God's Word is the highway of the supernatural of God.

Another illustration of walking in God's holiness: People can let their eyes (or any other body part) look at unholy things; but this will blind them from seeing blinded eyes opening, the dead rising, deaf ears hearing, incurable diseases cured, deformed things being recreated—we choose what we want to see. If we choose to see unholiness, we will be blinded from seeing God's glorious power at work.

First Thessalonians 5:22 teaches us plainly to, "Abstain from all appearance of evil." If we allow even a little bit of evil in our lives, we actually allow demon spirits to enter into our lives. When demon spirits come, they never come alone; they bring other demon spirits that are much worse than they are.

The psalmist knew this truth, and he wrote about it in Psalm 101:3, "I will set no wicked thing before mine eyes: I hate the work of them that turn aside; it shall not cleave to me." The Hebrew word for wicked is *bel-e-yah-a* meaning worthless. Many times there are things in this life that are absolute time stealers, and they are worthless. At the same time, we Christians need to enjoy life.

Enjoy Life!

It was about two years after Kenneth Hagin Sr. passed away, that I had the privilege of being translated to Heaven into a large coliseum-type of room. It looked like an old Roman coliseum, and within it many of the major Christian ministries that have ever lived were represented. It appeared to be a ministers' conference. I saw Brother Hagin up toward the top seating section, pretty much by himself. I went up to him, knowing in my spirit that he had insight into my life and ministry, because he was in Heaven.

For many, many years (maybe as many as 30 years), I have strongly perceived and believed that the Lord has called me into the last days signs and wonders ministry. However, up to that time, the struggle was much more than what I liked. So I went up to Brother Hagin and asked him, "Brother Hagin, is it true that my calling from God is to be a last days signs and wonders minister"?

He put one of his hands upon my shoulder and looked me in the eyes and said, "Yes, but what you need to do is learn to enjoy life." Many times ministers get so involved in trying to make ministry things happen that we let years go by without enjoying life the way the Lord wants us to.

God made a beautiful world and many beautiful things for all of us to enjoy. He did not intend for us to pray and read our Bibles in solitude all day long year after year and not enjoy His creation. He wants us to enjoy His wonderful Kingdom on earth and the wonderful things of life.

CHAPTER 7

Humility Before Honor

This following encounter with Jesus in the flesh caused me to understand some extremely powerful doctrines of God. Number 1, God is no respecter of persons. Number 2, Humility truly goes before honor. Number 3, We must be cautious how we treat strangers as we could be talking to Jesus or an angel (see Acts 10:34; Prov. 15:33; Heb. 13:2).

In October 1979, Donna and I were pastoring a church in Taylor, Texas. I had my pilot's license to fly small planes, so one day we rented a small 151-Cherokee Warrior plane, and we flew to Fort Worth, Texas, for a ministers' meeting where Kenneth Hagin Sr. was going to be speaking.

It was a Friday morning, October 5, 1979, and about 10 A.M. Brother Hagin was getting ready to minister. However, as he got up to speak, it was very obvious that the Holy Spirit was speaking to him. He sort of stared off from his concern of being before us and was captured by Holy Spirit's presence speaking to him.

After a short period of time, he looked at the group of ministers in the audience and said something like, "The Lord just told me that everyone here is to turn around, and the first person you make eye contact with, pray that the person would have your anointing for ministry. And that person will pray for you to have his or her anointing for ministry."

Donna and I were at our usual spot all the way in the back where the least important ministries sat. I did as Brother Hagin said. I turned around and there were about six rows of seats in back of us empty except one man all the way in the back to my left. He was dressed in a grey, khaki worker's uniform. He was about 6 feet tall with a Roman-looking haircut. It was obvious that he was a janitor or maintenance man who slipped in to see what was going on.

I had already spent years (and continued to do so for many, many years) being a pastor and the janitor of the church and doing jobs like cleaning out cow manure from barns, so I had *no* interest whatsoever of having a janitor's anointing.

I noticed the Janitor locked eyes with me in an extremely kind and gentle way, not pushy at all. However, I figured He would understand, as all the ministers there were wearing very nice suits and really looked the part.

I believe that we should dress nicely as the Bible plainly teaches that whatsoever we do in word or deed, do it as unto the Lord (see Col. 3:17, 23). So when we come to church we need to dress like we are coming to the Lord's House. It is true that 100 percent of the people in the world who get an invitation to visit the White House in the United States would sacrifice to buy a nice suit to wear. What is more important, the White House or God's House. Now if I'm going to feed hogs, I wear jeans and a shirt; but if I am going to feed God's children, the King's kids, I'm going to wear a nice suit.

Another train of thought that is true is this: When people have legal problems, they go to a lawyer. If they walked into the lawyer's office and he or she was wearing jeans and a work shirt, they would not use that lawyer. By lack of proper attire, the lawyer does not show professionalism and would make people think they would not receive proper counsel. What is more important—natural, temporal concerns or eternal concerns?

When I attend a church service, I am responsible by God to give eternal, divine counsel, and I must look the part. Even Jesus said, "…out of the abundance of the heart the mouth speaketh" (Matt. 12:34). Clearly Jesus was teaching us that whatever is in our hearts, our spirits, will be manifest in the natural. If we have a spirit of compromise in our spirits, it will show in our clothing, in our bodies, and our speech.

We ministers must not surrender to a demon of compromise regardless of what the rest of the world is doing. If we surrender to a small demon of compromise, we will allow other demons into our lives. If we compromise, we will not see the power of God in our lives and ministries.

As you read on in this chapter, you may think, *Well, Jesus was not dressed up in the finest suit of the day at this meeting; He came dressed as a janitor.*

However, if you study the life of Jesus, you will find He wore the best that money could buy in His day. He wore a garment that was so expensive that the Roman soldiers who crucified Him wanted it. They were gambling to try to get it. Study the garment that Jesus wore, and you'll find this to be true.

God many times throughout Scriptures uses different manifestations of simplicity to find out if the person will choose to love and respect people who are less fortunate, and that is why He comes in the form of a servant, like He did with the two disciples in Mark 16:12.

Back to the ministers' meeting in Fort Worth: when I saw that it was only a Janitor who was behind me, I turned back around and looked for some great minister to make eye contact with me. I remember this as if it were yesterday. I cried out in my spirit, *Oh Lord, please let one of these great ministers of the day turn and look at me. I really would love to have their anointing.* However, no one looked my way; they didn't want a ministry of very little value in the back seat to pray for them. They did not want that kind of anointing.

So I began to look to the right and to the left, thinking this Janitor knows that I am a minister and I need a minister's anointing, not a janitor's anointing; He would certainly understand if I go to a minister to exchange anointings.

There were about 1,500 ministers there representing many great ministries of the day. So I thought, *Well, there are a lot of ministers who have fine suits on that are sitting not too far in front of us and some to the left and right; and they look very successful. Maybe one of these guys will turn around and make eye contact with me, so I can have a successful ministry's anointing upon me.* However, not one turned around toward my direction. So I looked around me, and again not one looked my way. So I did what Brother Hagin said, I turned around to the empty seats, where the Janitor was sitting.

As soon as I turned around, I saw that the Janitor was still standing in the same place and He gently made eye contact with me again.

I thought in my mind, *Dear Lord, I am in the ministry. Lord, I always have to go where no one else goes and do what no other ministry will do; can I at least have a successful minister pray for me?*

However, this Man kept looking at me with a very humble and mild manner. I thought, *Lord, please allow at least one of these guys to the right or left of me look at me while I walk toward this Guy.* He was about 30 to 40 feet away from me, all the way in the back where no one else was sitting.

Then I thought, *OK Lord, I will go back and pray for this Guy, who no one else wants to pray for. Once again, I will do what no other minister wants to do.* In my mind I was saying, if perhaps one of these ministers near me who is dressed like a minister of the day would happen to make eye contact with me, this Man will understand as I go to that other person. However, it was like the Red Sea parting, everyone to the right and left dispersed, and it was only me and this Man in work clothes already mentioned several time before.

So we came together and held hands and began to pray. We both prayed; His prayer was so soft that I do not know what He said. But as He prayed, the power of God came from Him stronger than I have ever felt in my life. I've worked many times over the years with electricity and have been shocked by it often. But this was at least ten times stronger, yet it did not hurt.

This power went from my hands up into my shoulders and into my body, and I was elevated off the ground about 2-6 inches; it's hard to know for sure as God's power was so strong that all physical awareness was almost gone, if not all gone. At the time, I thought this power was probably coming from me, as this Man was just a janitor.

After He prayed for me and I came back down to the floor, which was only about three or four seconds. I did not look Him in the face for some reason. But instead I turned around and started walking back toward my seat. I only took a few steps, maybe three, and I turned back around to look at the Janitor, but He was totally gone. The closest door was about 40 feet away, and it would have been totally impossible for Him to have even run that fast to get out of the convention center. I knew I received a supernatural prayer and believed then and for many, many years that it was an angel.

This was the most influential, most divinely powerful prayer that I have ever received. His prayer supernaturally and totally captivated my spirit, mind, and body.

I thought I wanted the best, most successful minister in the place to pray for me; but instead, I got a Person who was better than all of the ministers; better than all of the ministries on the face of the earth. An angel of God came to me in the manifestation of a human in physical form and prayed for me; just like it says in Hebrews 13:2, "Be not forgetful to entertain strangers; for thereby some have entertained angels unawares."

I noticed from that day forward, that *if I would live in humility, I had a greater anointing on my life than I had ever had before.*

For example, not long after that experience, I went to a hospital to pray for a lady in the church who had died. There was a gentle boldness about me. I got into the hospital elevator and the two morticians from the town were in the same elevator. I asked them what they were there for. And they told me they were there to pick up this same lady's body. Then they asked me why I was there, and I told them I was there to raise this lady from the dead. Although the morticians were white men, they became even more white.

The elevator was full, and the next stop must have been a busy floor, because everyone got out of the elevator. When we got to the lady's room, the two morticians waited outside while I went in and raised her from the dead in the name of Jesus.

I could tell many, many stories about how my ministry changed because of having this heavenly being pray for me.

Proverbs 18:12 says, "Before destruction the heart of man is haughty, and *before honor is humility.*"

Proverbs 22:4 says, "By humility and the fear of the Lord are riches, and honor, and life."

James 4:10 says, "Humble yourselves in the sight of the Lord, and He shall lift you up."

If we will do what we have to do to humble ourselves—even when no one else is looking—God will honor us. God will cause great riches and the greatest of lifestyles to come into our lives.

The way up, is the way down.

The Spring of 2008

From that time until the Tuesday morning of March 25, 2008, if I ever thought about this experience or ever told anyone, I always thought and told people that this janitor was an angel. What an awesome experience it was to have an angel pray for me.

On March 25, 2008, I was reading my Bible as I do every morning. Mark 16:12 was part of the Bible reading. As I read it, it was as if the whole page lit up with God's glory. And then I perceived the Lord say to me, "That was Me who prayed for you in Fort Worth, Texas." I did not hear Him audibly or see Him physically, but it was more real than anything in this natural world. Because the realm of God is spiritual, it is divine, it is of the eternal world and much more real than anything in this natural world.

When He said that to me, a tangible anointing from the Lord came all over my body. I knew that the Lord spoke to me. The room was filled with the presence of the Lord and His Shekinah glory.

In Luke 24:13-34 and Mark 16:9-12 you will find the story of Jesus appearing to two of His followers after He had been crucified and raised from the dead. In Mark 16:12, it says that Jesus appeared in another form unto the two of them. As you study this passage, you find that the two did not know it was Jesus because Jesus appeared in another form.

The word form in the Greek in this passage is *morph*, which means nature. This same Greek word is also used in Philippians 2:7, "But made Himself of no reputation, and took upon Him the *form* [Greek word: *morphe*] of a servant, and was made in the likeness of men."

I could not remember the exact date, so I asked the Lord just now while writing (June 9, 2010 at 8:40 A.M.), "When did You speak to me and tell me that it was You who prayed for me at Fort Worth, Texas?" Then the Lord spoke so clearly to me and said it was March 25, 2008, and that was a Tuesday morning. I was only going to put the year down as I was not sure about the right date. However, I looked it up on the perpetual calendar and this date was, of course, a Tuesday.

Again, by an undeniable, unforgettable experience of being in the very presence of Jesus, my life and ministry were changed.

I learned to make sure that I never overlook one human

being. *Everyone* is extremely valuable and precious to the Lord. God does not see a mass of people, He sees individuals.

I also learned that humility is what God is looking for, not talent or any other thing.

I learned that Jesus and angels are walking among us in human form, as Hebrews 13:2 plainly teaches.

CHAPTER 8

Seeing With Your Spiritual Eyes

This next vision of Jesus helped me to actually see how God's power works in the spirit world. It also showed me how powerful our born-again spirits are.

It was about 1982 when I invited a preacher I knew of for several years, to come to our church. This man was about 47 years of age at that time and lived with one of God's wonders.

When he was a young boy about the age of 12, Ronald lived in the country and was playing with a piece of sharp barbed wire. He was swinging it around his head and it hit one of his eyes, tearing his eye ball out of his head. When it healed, the doctors fitted him for a plastic eye.

He went to a church that believed in miracles and healing, and they had a lady evangelist come to their church to hold a revival. Ronald was sitting near the front of the church, and in one of the services the lady saw Ronald and noticed his eye looked different. She thought he had a cold or something minor like that wrong with his eye.

She went to Ronald and said something like, "God is going to give you a miracle and heal your eye, you will not have anything wrong with it, and you will see perfectly." So when the evangelist prayed for Ronald, he simply released his faith and began to see perfectly with the glass eye. From that time on, Ronald could see perfectly with the plastic eye—or without it.

He went from church to church and various places with a powerful message, and then he would have people come forward and put a cloth patch over his natural eye, and then wrap about 20 feet of bandage over the patch. Then he would take out his plastic eye and have people bring him their driver's licenses or whatever they wanted him to read, and he would read it perfectly. He would then walk around the church preaching and praying for people.

Ronald was even on the Phil Donahue Show and a few other shows like that. I remember an atheist eye doctor who was on one of the shows, and he examined Ronald's eye. He said it was a miracle and received the Lord Jesus as his Savior.

About one week before Ronald came to our church in Wentzville, Missouri, I went to bed and fell asleep. During the night session, I saw Jesus in a vision of the night, a dream. Jesus came up to me and said, "Mel, I want to show you how Ronald sees." We walked a little while, and then I saw Ronald standing about 15 feet away. Ronald was standing so we could see the side of his face. Jesus said, "Look at his temple area, deep inside his head."

At this time it was obvious that Jesus had opened up my

understanding so I could see in the spirit world. When I looked where Jesus told me to look, I notice there was a bright light that was brighter than the noonday sun; it was the Shekinah glory of God in Ronald's head where Jesus told me to look, and it was about the size of a dime. Jesus then said, "Ronald sees from his spiritual eye."

In this vision, Ronald turned to look at something through that spiritual eye and a beam that looked like a laser beam, with the same forces and brightness of his spiritual eye, went forth from his spiritual eye to whatever he wanted to see. It was like a laser beam coming from the inside of his head from the base of that round piece of God's glory, that was about the size of a dime.

Jesus said again, "Ronald sees out of his spiritual eye."

This vision of Jesus and what He showed me has helped me believe God for great miracles. Since then, I've met people who did not have eyes; I have prayed for them, and they received their sight. The first time this happened I was in India in 1992. I was conducting a miracle crusade in Shamoga, and a boy of about 12 years of age had some kind of white substance filling and hanging from in his eye sockets; it would bounce up and down touching his face, sort of like chicken fat hanging from his eyes about 1½- to 2 inches long

When I saw him, my heart cried out to the Lord with compassion for the boy. He was the first one I called up on the platform. I prayed with my whole heart, and he began to see with good vision. It appeared that he could see normally, as he was seeing things and then describing them with accuracy. The crowd was excited, and when the praising of the Lord stopped, I thought, *I want to see those new, recreated eyes.* When I looked at the little boy, the globby substance was still there, but the boy could see fine. God calls those things that are not even as though they were (see Rom. 4:17). Dan F. of Maryland Heights, Missouri, was there with me and saw this miracle of God.

CHAPTER 9

Pray With Your Whole Heart

I will not spend a lot of time on this next visitation of Jesus as I wrote a whole book just about this experience titled *Releasing God's Anointing.*

This experience also changed the course of my life and my ministry. It was very important to me, as it helped me to have divine confidence to pray for any type of situation.

Friday evening September 24, 1984, I went to sleep; and during the night session, by a vision I went into our next Sunday's church service. I was preaching and noticed someone tapped me on the right shoulder. I turned to see who it was, and it was Jesus. He said to me, "Mel, see that red-headed lady? She has this type of a problem in her body. If you will pray with your whole heart, My anointing will go into her, and she will be instantly healed."

He then said, "If you will learn to pray with your whole heart, My anointing will always go into people, and there will always be an instant manifestation."

When Jesus said that, I could easily write a 500-page book of what He said, as information by volumes went into my spirit and mind. However, I am not a detailed person. I like to stick to the major points and go on. So I simply wrote a small book that gets to the point with simplicity. Children read my book and they are able to yield to the Gifts of the Holy Spirit and pray for people, and miracles instantly manifest. I've seen this in person.

The information that came to me from Jesus caused me to know that if I am single-minded, God's anointing will always go into people. I understood that being single-minded means to: Number 1, focus on the problem disappearing. Number 2, focus on that area receiving God's anointing. Number 3, focus on getting the person to do something that they could not do or was difficult to do before.

When Jesus told me that His anointing would always go into people and there would be a manifestation of His power, I also understood that the people receiving had to do the same thing. They had to focus on the problem going away, focus on surrendering to God's anointing, and focus on doing something that they could not do or was difficult to do before.

In the Greek language, the words surrender, yield, accept, and relax are coequal terms. So I tell people to relax in the area where they need a miracle, understanding that relaxing is the same word in the Greek for surrendering to God's anointing. People can relate to relaxing much easier than surrendering.

Note: Keep in mind when Jesus or an angel appears to

you, many times they do not have to say anything and a great deal of information is transmitted into your mind and spirit. And then sometimes they can say very little, yet much information is transmitted into your mind or spirit. God's world is supernatural.

It is one thing to give someone something, but it is another thing for a person to accept it; and then another thing for a person to know how to receive it.

However, these simple words that I have given to you will cause instant manifestation for any kind of miracle in the Bible that you have ever read about. I've seen hundreds of totally blind eyes open, deaf ears open, incurable pain leave, incurable diseases leave, many deformed bodies recreate— and even a few corpses rise to life again.

So that Sunday morning after the night vision of Jesus, I got up to preach after the song service. As I looked into the congregation, to my left about three chairs back and about two chairs to the left of the center row, there was the red-headed lady I had seen that previous Friday night in the vision. Everything in the service was the same, except Jesus did not appear and tap me on the right shoulder.

So I finished my message and did exactly what Jesus told me to do in the vision. The lady said that was exactly what was wrong with her. I did as Jesus instructed me, and the lady said she was instantly healed by God's power. I saw the lady about ten years after this miracle, and she told me that she was still healed in that area of her body. Her name is Marine P. and lives in the O'Fallon, Missouri area, the last I heard.

A major lesson I've learned from the Lord and the Holy Scriptures is: if it isn't easy enough that a child cannot do it, then it isn't of God (see Matt. 18:3). Psalm 119:130 says, "The entrance of Thy words giveth light; it giveth understanding unto the simple."

If you would like more in-depth study on this particular vision; please read my book *Releasing God's Anointing*.

CHAPTER 10

Mansion in Glory

This visitation of Jesus in Heaven caused me to know that everything we do for the Lord is not forgotten by Him, and He blesses us beyond our imagination for the work we do for Him.

Hebrews 6:10 says, "For God is not unrighteous to forget your work and labor of love, which ye have shewed toward His name, in that ye have ministered to the saints, and do minister."

So true!

It was in the fall of 1984 when Donna and I were building Agape Church on 140 N. Point Prairie Street in Wentzville, Missouri. We were actually building it with our own hands. In faith we bought five acres of ground; I rented a bulldozer, and I personally started bulldozing the land to get it ready to construct a building that would seat 1,200 people in the auditorium. The building would have about 18,000 square feet.

We hired others to do the concrete work, electric, plumbing work, and build the shell. I was physically working from early morning until late in the night, day after day. We started in the fall of '84 and we were in the building by the end of January 1985 for our first service.

I share that to let you know how much physical work we were doing. Sometimes a few of the men from the church would stop by after they would get off work to help me. The most we ever had at one time would be maybe eight guys. Many times I would be there all day and into the night by myself. I was not complaining; in fact, I was thrilled that I could do something of this caliber for the Lord.

Late that fall I went to sleep; and during the night session, I went to Heaven. As soon as I got there, I saw Jesus. He had a big smile on His face and said, "Mel, I want to show you what I am doing for you, just for what you're doing for Me right now in Wentzville." We walked up a beautiful grassy hill, and then the landscape sort of leveled out, then started to slope downhill just a little. As soon as we reached the top of the hill, I saw a huge mansion. It looked about 400 feet wide, facing the front elevation.

Yes, the Bible is true where Jesus said in John 14:2, "In my Father's house are many mansions: if it were not so, I would have told you. I go to prepare a place for you."

The front elevation was already completed. Jesus said, "This is your house for what you're doing for Me right now." The house was a mansion beyond anything I've ever seen. The front had some type of a brown wood that I have never seen. However, it was obvious that Jesus knew me better than I do, as this mansion was totally satisfying to me.

I am really not much of a person for physical things, but this was a gift from Jesus, and that meant a lot. We walked down to the house and went inside. The front entry was about 75 feet deep and about that wide. I noticed that a rose (my favorite flower) was imbedded in a wall on the right side. Next to the rose, on the left side was a door that went into one of the rooms of the mansion. However, I only got to see the front elevation and the front entry, and then the vision was over.

Inside the entry was beautiful, but the thing I remember most was the people in the front entry who were working on the mansion. They were extremely joyful and it was obvious that they knew me very well. However, I did not know any of them at all.

I've been to Heaven a few times, and I have seen people there that I know. For example, Donna and I have children we lost during her pregnancies. The last child went full term but did not live very long. We knew she was a little girl, the others we never knew the gender as they were lost in early pregnancy.

However, we were attached to this little girl because she was full term and was born. Her name is Celestial Dawn Bond, and she died February 15, 1978. Over the years I've had the privilege of watching her grow up. Sometimes I would not see her for a few years. But I've seen her during some of the major growing periods of her life. About three years ago was the last time I saw her, and that was the only time she ever spoke to me.

So many times in Heaven, when I see people I know, they say very little or nothing, as if they are not supposed to say anything to me. I sense it is because God wants us to walk and live by faith; and these people could give us supernatural information. However, the last time I saw Celestial, she came up to me and hugged me and put her head on my chest and said, "Hello, Dad." When she did that, there was such an awesome anointing of God that came on me. And every time I think of this event, that anointing comes back. It causes me to long for Heaven. This experience also gives me a stronger anointing to live for the Lord.

Getting back to Jesus showing me my mansion in Heaven: as I think back on this experience of seeing Jesus and Him taking me to see the mansion He is building for me, it gives me supernatural encouragement. I am not interested in things and never have been, but if I get a rock from someone precious to me, it will be valued all the days of my life, and how much more if Jesus gives me something.

I have a rock about the size of a silver dollar that an Indian lady by the name of Choctaw gave me several years ago and it is on my desk. I will keep it there the rest of my life as a memento of her. She is a precious lady.

You can rest assured that the Lord knows everything you do for Him, and He will honor you for your work beyond your fondest dreams.

Hebrews 6:10 says, "For God is not unrighteous to forget

your work and labor of love, which ye have shewed toward His name, in that ye have ministered to the saints, and do minister."

This vision of the Lord has caused a supernatural encouragement to come to me when I am going through hard times. We all have times when it seems like no one cares, like all of the good we do is unnoticed. But an experience like this—knowing it was a valid, divine, scriptural experience that God ordained—gives a person supernatural encouragement, peace in the midst of the worst storms, and joy when the natural world presents no reason whatsoever for you to have joy.

CHAPTER 11

The Importance of Your Life

This visitation of Jesus caused me to know that every human's life is ordained with a divine purpose; and many people can be blessed in this life, because of our lives. Also, many people will avoid horrible attacks of the devil and even avoid hell because of our lives.

This vision caused me to know of God's great depths of His great love that He has for every human.

The year 1990 was one of the worst, if not *the* worst, years of my life. I really believe the devil did everything he could to make me miserable, to ruin my life—he even tried to kill me. I believe this was his great attempt to stop Donna's and my ministry. That year several relatives died and a few people from our church who were close to us died. There were several horrible attacks against Donna and I personally as well as against our family—attacks beyond what I could ever talk about.

I was very discouraged. Then one evening after I went to

bed and during the night session, I went to Heaven. While I was there, I saw some people I knew and some that knew me and seemed to know a lot about me and my life on earth. I told everyone there that I'd had enough problems and disappointments, and I was going to stay in Heaven this time; I was not going back to earth. At the time, I was 39 years of age, but I was totally finished with life on earth.

It was as if I was in Heaven for two days. The Bible does say in Second Peter 3:8, "But, beloved, be not ignorant of this one thing, that one day is with the Lord as a thousand years, and a thousand years as one day." Time in Heaven and with God is much different from time as we know it here on earth.

So the second day, I was walking down a street, extremely happy. Being in Heaven exudes a feeling of tranquility, a fulfillment of life beyond the natural human being's thinking. We can have this same tranquil lifestyle on earth if we follow some basic biblical truths. Joshua 1:8 does it for you; read it carefully.

The things of Heaven, the mansions, the splendor, etc. do not make Heaven, Heaven. Rather, it is the divine atmosphere of contentment. As I was walking down this street, I heard someone call my name. I turned around to see Jesus about 200 feet behind me. I began to gently run toward Him and He did the same. Jesus had this great, warm and friendly smile. I really do not have the adequate words to describe the divinity that is placed in a person's life when looking into the eyes of Jesus.

There is such a warm love, a deep caring, a look that

fills you with a feeling and a perception of being the most important person in all of existence. You draw supernatural strength knowing God is 100 percent for you. You are overwhelmed with divinity just by looking into His eyes. Actually, there are no human words to fully describe the sensational, the supernatural feeling and perception that a person gets just by looking into Jesus' eyes. It will change you forever.

To say it most accurately, no person can describe with human words the experience of looking into Jesus eyes; it can only be experienced.

Again I say that the experience of being in Jesus' presence and looking into His eyes caused me to feel like I was the most important person in all of existence to Jesus.

Please know this: Jesus feels the exact same way about every human being. Somehow every person is the most important person in all of existence to the Lord.

It was very evident that He was extremely happy to see me; as soon as we reached each other, we embraced as two best friends would. He made me feel as if I was the best friend He ever had. In a very real, supernatural way, everyone is His best friend in the same way.

He put His left arm over my right shoulder, and we began to walk down the street together. He asked me how I was doing, not to just make conversation; I could perceive deep inside me, that Jesus was truly interested in anything that I was interested in. I told Him I was very happy now, and that I loved Heaven. He then said, "Mel, I heard that you are not going back this time?" I looked up at Him with discouragement in my heart, thinking, *He is going to make me go back. And I really don't want to go back. I love my wife very much, and my children, and parents, and brother and sisters, but the agony seems too great with all of the things I have been facing on earth and am still facing.*

Jesus looked at me with a big smile and said, "Don't be discouraged; if you do not want to go back, I will not make you. The decision is yours!" I was very relieved. Then Jesus looked at me and said, "Before you make up your mind, I want to show you something." We continued walking straight ahead; it seemed like a long distance, but it also seemed as if we only took a step or two until we came to what seemed like the edge of Heaven and we stopped.

There were clouds in front of us and they began to part in the center making a hole that showed the earth beneath. I was able to see into the future and see the tribulation period on the earth. I saw the earth in a disastrous state. I saw people running in different directions with their clothes dirty and torn. It was as if changing clothes was not important at all. I saw in just this one scene thousands of people screaming and crying in torment, and I knew there were millions of other people in other areas facing the same situation.

Then I saw someone extremely dear to me, someone I thought would never go through the tribulation period. This person was crying with tears streaming down her face. She was in torment, great torment. The scene gripped my heart so deeply. Then Jesus said to me, "If you stay, you cannot help her or others."

As I have said before, in the spirit world, volumes of information can be transmitted into one's mind and spirit from Jesus or an angel with only a few words, or maybe no words at all. I knew beyond all reasoning that Jesus was saying that family members and other people I loved dearly and millions of other people would go through the tribulation period and many into hell if I selfishly decided to stay in Heaven.

When Jesus said that, and after seeing that scene, I immediately said, "I have to go back!" At that moment, I woke up in my bed.

I know that if I would have made up my mind to stay in Heaven that my body would have died with medical science saying they could find no natural causes. This happens all of the time. James 2:26 says, "For as the body without the spirit is dead, so faith without works is dead also." When people decide in the spirit that they do not want to live any longer, their spirits leave their bodies, and the body cannot live without the spirit living inside the body. This is one of the reasons that throughout the Scriptures the word heart is used in reference to the human spirit.

I found out what the apostle Paul meant in Philippians 1:23-24, "For I am in a strait betwixt two, having a desire to depart, and to be with Christ; which is far better: Nevertheless to abide in the flesh is more needful for you."

This vision has supernaturally helped me to go to places where it is extremely uncomfortable to win people to the Lord Jesus. It has caused me to continue on, even after years of seeing defeat in many areas. It has helped me stay focused on winning the lost for the Lord Jesus.

Since this vision, Donna and I have won at least 900,000 people to the Lord, and we are convinced that there are many more we will win to the Lord—as well as encourage, train, and love into a deeper relationship with the Lord.

CHAPTER 12

Jesus, the Horn of Salvation

The next experience that I'm going to share of seeing Jesus in Heaven, caused me to have more confidence in the love and miracle-working power of God. It has caused me to know that holiness is a major factor that must be established in people's lives, if they want to flow with the supernatural of God. Romans 1:4 teaches us plainly that Jesus was declared to be the Son of God with power (this word power is the Greek word *dunamis,* which is translated as the greatest miracle-working power of God.

Jesus is our example, and we must follow His life's pattern.

I am very much aware of the grace of God. I am not saying that we need to get into religious works to try to earn God's miracle-working power, as this is impossible because it has already been given to every human being (see 2 Pet. 1:3-4; Rom. 8:32). But if we choose to let sin stay in our lives, it gives satan rights to blind us.

Second Corinthians 4:3-4 says, "But if our gospel be hid,

it is hid to them that are lost. In whom the god of this world hath blinded the minds of them which believe not, lest the light of the glorious gospel of Christ, who is the image of God, should shine unto them."

If we have sin in our lives, we will be blinded by satan. It will not stop the blessings of God; we simply will not be able to use them, because we cannot see them. A good example of this is the one given previously about giving a blind person a car to drive.

May 26, 1999 was a Wednesday, and that evening I went to bed and went to sleep. During the night session, I went to Heaven. I was immediately standing in a street in Heaven and noticed a crowd, which looked like about 150 people at the most. The crowd was standing on a little bit of a slope to the right of the street, so I could see that it was Jesus who was speaking to this group of people. He was very calm, cheerful, and not loud at all.

I used to think if I was not yelling, I was not preaching properly. I guess that was because of my Full Gospel background. I still think it is OK to have some emotion in our speech from time to time, but we need to make sure that we never confuse emotionalism with the anointing of God.

Every time I've seen Jesus, He was never yelling, He was always very loving, very kind and soft-spoken. And this time, it was the first time I had ever heard Him preach or teach to a group of people. His demeanor was the same: calm, loving, and soft-spoken.

I wish I could remember what Jesus was speaking about;

even immediately after this experience, I could not remember what He was speaking about. It was evident that Jesus did not want me to remember anything other than what I was there for.

While He was speaking, He stopped to give someone in the crowd a fan. I knew the fan was symbolic of an anointing for a special ministry on the earth. The fan was very beautiful. As I stood there watching Jesus give this beautiful fan to this person, I thought, *I wish Jesus would have given me that fan.*

It really wouldn't matter what Jesus gave me, just getting something, anything from Him would be extremely awesome. It was like Jesus knew exactly what I was thinking, and He stopped again in the middle of His sermon and stooped down and picked up a beautiful horn. It was not as beautiful as the fan, but it was beautiful.

Then He called out my name. Having Jesus call out your name is quite an experience. Then He started walking toward me with a great smile on His face. He said, "Mel, I want to give you My Horn of Salvation." I was overwhelmed with joy. I noticed as He handed it to me that it had a tag on it; it looked like a price tag. The writing on the tag seemed to be Hebrew or Greek, but I had no knowledge of what it meant; but I knew that it meant there was a price to pay to have Jesus' Horn of Salvation.

At that time I had studied the Bible many, many times as well as researching more words and verses in the Greek and Hebrew than I could possibly calculate or remember. But I had no idea what the Horn of Salvation meant, much less Jesus' Horn of Salvation. So I began to look up every verse in the Bible that mentioned the Horn of Salvation, or any verses that related to the Horn of Salvation.

And this is what I found: Jesus' Horn of Salvation is the greatest miracle-working power of God. Let me say this before I go any further, I am not any more special than anyone else on the earth. God has already given every human being everything that pertains to *God-likeness* (see 2 Peter 1:3-4). So every human being has Jesus' Horn of Salvation. I simply must have needed more assurance at the time and that must have been the purpose of God initiating this vision.

Let's look at the Horn of Salvation in Luke 1:69, "And hath raised up an horn of salvation for us in the house of his servant David." The word salvation in this passage is the Greek word *sōtēria*. This word is coequally rendered as: *rescue* or *safety* (physically or morally)—deliver, health, salvation, save, saving, or *protect,* heal, preserve, do well, be (make) whole.

As you study the times of Jesus, you find that the people used horns to announce important events. And Jesus most definitely hosted the greatest events that could possibly happen on earth. He opened blinded eyes, opened deaf ears, and released the power of God so that people who were maimed (missing body parts) where made whole (see Matt. 15:30); He also raised the dead, just to list a few things that Jesus did.

First Samuel 2:10 says, "The adversaries of the Lord

shall be broken to pieces; out of heaven shall He thunder upon them: the Lord shall judge the ends of the earth; and He shall give strength unto His King, and exalt *the horn of His anointed.*" The Scriptures declare the strength and the almightiness of God exalting the horn of His anointed.

The Hebrew word for horn in this passage is *qeren,* which means *projecting,* a *ray* (of light); figuratively *power.*

The phrase in this passage, "of His anointed," is one word in the Hebrew, *mashiyach.* The fuller meaning of this word in the Hebrew is *anointed;* usually a *consecrated* person (as a king, priest, or saint); specifically the *Messiah*—anointed, Messiah.

Most definitely Jesus broke to pieces His adversaries; and He gave strength to kings and queens—and we all are now kings and queens because of the work of Jesus. Notice Romans 5:17, "For by one man's offence death reigned by one: much more they which receive abundance of grace and of the gift of righteousness shall *reign* in life by One, Jesus Christ." Keep in mind the word reign in this verse is rendered in the Greek as: to rule and reign as a king or queen. And God did this as His anointed one, Jesus the Messiah displayed the Horn of His Salvation.

Habakkuk 3:4 says, "And His brightness was as the light; He had horns coming out of His hand: and there was the hiding of His power."

The Hebrew word for horn is the same Hebrew word

rendered as horn in First Samuel 2:10. Notice Habakkuk 3:4 in the Amplified version of the Bible reads that, "His [Jesus'] brightness was like the sunlight; rays streamed from His hand, and there [in the sunlike splendor] was the hiding place of His power."

Very simply, Jesus' Horn of Salvation is the sunlight splendor that beams from Him, and there in that sunlight splendor is the hiding place of God's greatest power!

Keep in mind that as He is, so are we in this world! (See First John 4:17.)

The Price Tag

I perceive the price tag is living a life of holiness. Romans 1:4 is talking about Jesus when it says, "And declared to be the Son of God with power, according to the spirit of holiness...."

The word declared in this passage is the Greek word *horizō,* which means ordain. Keep in mind that ordination is the highest order of sanctioning or approving that any organization or power can place on someone.

The word power in this passage is the Greek word *dunamis,* which means specifically miraculous *power* (usually by implication a *miracle* itself), (worker of) miracle (-s), power.

Jesus was ordained, was approved of God by the highest standards in all existence to be the Son of God, because Jesus lived a holy life! First John 4:17 says that as He is, so are we in this world!

Keep in mind that holiness is the most pleasurable, most fulfilling, most satisfying, most exciting way to live. The flesh has to be taught to live this way, as the flesh is crazy.

After Jesus gave me His Horn of Salvation, I woke up and it was about 5:15 A.M.

At that time in my life, I had been raising elk for about six years. I knew one of my cows was due with a calf, so I went over to the acreage where I kept the elk and in the birthing lot I found a baby bull calf that was just born no more than 30 minutes earlier. This was the first bull calf to have ever been born on my farm. I am totally convinced this bull calf was a confirmation of the vision I just had of Jesus only minutes earlier. Only bull elk grow horns. The female elk do not grow horns. By my calculation, this bull calf was born at exactly the same time that Jesus gave me His Horn of Salvation.

The registration paper of this bull calf is inserted on the following page for your review. Notice the date of birth: May 27, 1999.

Since this experience on May 27, 1999, I have seen some of the greatest, most awesome miracles, as well as hundreds of thousands of people accept Jesus as their Lord because of the miracles.

When people are in an atmosphere where such great miracles take place, not only are they brought to tears by the greatness of God's miracle-working power, but there is a presence of God's love, compassion, and fullness so supreme that it makes Jesus irresistible.

Certificate of Registration **GOLD**

North American Elk Breeders Association

1708 N.Prairie View Rd PO Box 1640
Platte City, MO 64079   PH (816) 431-3605   FAX (816) 431-2705

REGISTRATION #: A12798   Registration Date: **01/10/2000**

This is to certify the pedigree of: **QUARRY DELUXE-7**   USDA NO.

Sex: **Male**	Date Calved: **05/27/1999**	Birth Date: **Actual**	Multi-Birth: **Single**
Ear Tag: **4**		Dual Tag:	Birth Type: **A.I.**
Microchip: **031018806**		Tattoo:	USDA Tag:

Present Owner: **3382-00**	Mel & Donna Bond	Herd # : **1087**	% Owned: **100%**
	Bond Elk Ranch 566 Bell Rd Wright City MO 63390		
Breeder: **3382-00**	Mel & Donna Bond	Herd # : **1087**	
	Bond Elk Ranch 566 Bell Rd Wright City MO 63390		
Previous Owner:		Herd # :	

PEDIGREE   REGISTERED

DNA Test Lab: **UCD**   Case # : **EK7355**   Test Date: **01/06/2000**   Result: **2**

Sire:

Sire: MAJESTICS ACE
E010637519
Dam:

Sire: QUARRY CREEK ACE (BLACKHAWK)   DNA: 1
E023317127
Sire:

Dam: FORTY FIVE, TAG W-62
E001592268
Dam:

Sire:

Sire: BIG DELUXE 957
E043957
Dam:

Dam:
A5939
Sire:

Dam:
E001768883
Dam:

* Owner supplied ancestor pedigree information is printed in italics on this certificate.
1 - DNA Profile   2 - DNA Matched to Sire   3 - DNA Matched to Dam   4 - DNA Matched to Sire & Dam

This is to certify that the animal and ancestors described in this
Certificate of Registration have been accepted for entry in the North
American Elk Breeders Association Herd Registry. This certificate
is issued in full reliance upon the truth of the statements contained
in the application for registration, breeders reports filed, blood test
results reported and in accordance with the rules and Regulations of
the NAEBA Registry and the By-Laws of the Association.

PRESIDENT

Date Issued: **01/11/2000**

In January 2000, I was conducting a miracle crusade in Chinadegau, Nicaragua. I always look for people with visible needs and have them brought up on the platform—things that people can see, like deformed bodies, etc. I am totally convinced that this last grand, final move of God will be a manifestation of signs and wonders that are clearly demonstrated—people will definitely see the miracle taking place in front of their eyes. First Corinthians 2:4-5 says, "And my speech and my preaching was not with enticing words of man's wisdom, but in demonstration of the Spirit and of power: that your faith should not stand in the wisdom of men, but in the power of God."

On that particular night, I asked the ushers to bring up to the platform people who were totally blind. Two ladies were brought up, and God's miracle power opened their eyes so they could see as normally as everyone else there. A lady brought her young daughter to the platform, who seemed to be about 7 years of age. The lady was crying and asking if my God could heal her daughter's eyes. The little girl's eyes looked very much like the little boy's eyes in India. The white substance filled her eye sockets but it wasn't globbing down on her face, as it had with the little boy. I told the lady all things were possible with my God! Gary Meador, who is now the founder and President of Rhema Bible College in Costa Rica, was my interpreter. Gary was born and raised in the United States and attended Rhema Bible College in Tulsa, Oklahoma. From there, he went on the mission field, married a Costa Rican lady, and is an interpreter for visiting pastors; he speaks excellent Spanish.

Gary was standing next to me as I prayed for the little girl. I had my eyes closed, as that is my custom, so I can focus more on what I am praying for without being distracted. On the plane going back home, Gary told me what he saw as I prayed. Gary said that as I prayed, there appeared two little white tornado-looking things that covered each of the girl's eyes. And when I stopped praying, the little tornadoes were gone and the little girl had two perfect brown eyes. The little girl began looking around and seeing things that a person could only see who had normal vision.

Eddie Rogers, a pastor in Georgia, was sitting on the platform with several other ministers from the U.S., and they all saw this miracle taking place. Recently when I was interviewed by Sid Roth on his television show, *It's Supernatural!*, Eddie Rogers was there to validate this little girl's miracle. If you go to the archives of Sid Roth's shows on the Internet, you will see and hear Brother Roger's testimony.

Dr. P.C. Nelson, (founder of Southwestern Bible School at Enid, Oklahoma in 1927) was a noted linguist. A secular magazine stated some 30 years ago that he was the leading authority of his day on Greek and the second-ranked authority on Hebrew. He could read and write 32 languages.

I sat in one of Brother Hagin's services and heard him make this statement: Dr. P.C. Nelson said that where John 14:12-14 says, "If you ask anything in my name, I will do it", in the English language we do not have a completely accurate translation for the phrase, "I will do it". He said that, though this is the strongest assurance that we have in our English language, more words would be needed to say exactly what Jesus was saying when He said, "I will do it". He said that in the Greek it basically says, "If you ask anything in my name, if it does not exist, I will make it for you!" And that verse came to pass that day!

In 2001, in Bogota, Columbia, South America, a little girl of about 8 months of age was brought onto the platform. The little girl had one leg that was about 1½ inches shorter than the other, which is quite a difference for a little baby. She was also born with her legs frozen at an angle of about 160 degrees. She was in a body cast to pull the legs together little by little. The doctors hoped to be able to pull the legs together by the time she was an adult. I prayed, and then took the body cast off. Her legs miraculously came together perfectly with both legs being the same length. This miracle we have on video. We do not show it openly as the little girl had no clothes on and the video is explicit.

In the mountains above Cualtla, Mexico, is an extremely poor village, and I went there to conduct a miracle service for a little church. Reverend Jorge Carrillo, the husband of America Carrillo of Cualtla, Mexico, was my interpreter. A young lady of about 13 years of age was born totally blind in one eye and that same side of her face was deformed. One side of her face was about 1½ to 2 inches lower than the other side of her face. In other words, one eye socket was about 1-2 inches lower than the other side.

As I prayed with my whole heart, the little girl's face was recreated, and she had perfect eyesight in both eyes.

Jesus Christ—the same yesterday, today, and forever!

CHAPTER 13

Jesus Wants to Appear to You!

The most awesome, prestigious honor is for Jesus to appear to you. It will change your life forever!

And I believe that He desires greatly to appear to every human being personally. And if He does, the very first moment you will know how extremely loved and important you are to Him.

Jesus Wants to Appear to You

To have Jesus appear to you is an awesome and an extremely divine privilege beyond any other privilege. And God has no favorites! Galatians 3:28 says, "There is neither Jew nor Greek, there is neither bond nor free, there is neither male nor female: for ye are all one in Christ Jesus."

What Jesus has done for one person, He will do for all! God respects all persons the same (see Acts 10:34).

In Psalm 95:2, the Bible gives us an invitation from God to see the Lord face-to-face in person; this verse declares, "Let us come before His *presence* with *thanksgiving....*"

In this passage, the word presence is the Hebrew word *paniym* and is rendered as: face, him (-self), person. The word thanksgiving is the Hebrew word *todah* meaning an *extension* of the hand, *adoration,* worshipers, confession, (sacrifice of) praise, thanks (-giving, offering).

I believe that the only way to worship or communicate with God is by and through His Word (see John 4:24; 14:6). So God is giving us a loving invitation to experience Jesus face-to-face in person *by putting strong emphasis on His Word.* Also, you can see there is a place of worship, as Psalm 95:2 clearly shows, that takes us into the very presence of Jesus; seeing Him face-to-face.

In Psalm 100:4 we again see God inviting us to come into the very presence of Jesus. This verse reads, "Enter into His gates with *thanksgiving,* and into His courts with *praise:* be thankful unto Him, and bless His name." The Hebrew word for *thanksgiving* is the same word thanksgiving in Psalm 95:2. The Hebrew word for praise is *thillah* meaning *laudation* of praise. The root word for this word is *halal,* coequally rendered as: to *shine;* hence to *make a show;* to *boast;* and thus to *be* (clamorously) *foolish;* to *rave;* causatively to *celebrate;* (make) boast (self), celebrate, fool (-ish, -ly), give [light], rage, shine). The Hebrew word for the phrase "be thankful" is *yadah.* This word is rendered also as: hold out *the hand;* physically to especially to *revere* or *worship* (with extended hands).

Again, another clear passage of being able to come into the very courtroom of Jesus is by praising Him with our whole hearts, being clamorously foolish in praising the Lord.

If you are in the very gates where Jesus lives, in the innermost court of the Lord, you absolutely will see Him!

Hebrews 4:16 gives us another wonderful invitation to see Jesus! This verse reads, *"Let us therefore come boldly unto the throne of grace, that we may obtain mercy, and find grace to help in time of need."* The word come in this passage is the Greek word *proserchomai,* translated as visit, approach, come enter.

If God is inviting us to come to His throne, who do you think you will see? Jesus, of course! "This Jesus hath God raised up.... Therefore being by the right hand of God.... The Lord said unto my Lord, Sit thou on My right hand" (Acts 2:32-34).

I've already shown you that the Holy Scriptures provide the way into the presence of Jesus (see John 4:24;14:6). So if you will do all of the things written in this book, you then can have boldness to get into the very presence of Jesus.

James 4:8 says, *"Draw nigh to God, and He will draw nigh to you."* The phrase used twice in this passage, "draw nigh," is the Greek word *eggizo,* which means: to make *near, approach,* be at hand, come near.

The decision is yours!

"Behold, I stand at the door, and knock: if any *man hear* My voice, and open the door, *I will come* in to him, and will sup with him, and he with Me" (Rev. 3:20). The phrase, "man hear" is one Greek word, which is *akouo ak-oo,* which means give audience, come. The phrase, "my voice" is one Greek word, which is *phone* and means *saying* or *language.* And the phrase in this passage, "I will come" is one Greek word, *eiserchomai,* meaning appear.

Putting all of this information together, clearly you can read this passage as saying: If we will give audience to God's language (His Word), Jesus will appear to us!

Psalm 37:4 says, "Delight thyself also in the Lord; and he shall give thee the desires of thine heart." If your desire is to see Jesus, continue delighting yourself in the Lord and His Word, and God will give you the desires of your heart!

If the desire of your heart is to see Jesus, and you are in the pathway (as described in this book), then Jesus will appear to you.

Mark 11:24 says, "Therefore I say unto you, What things soever ye desire, when ye pray, believe that ye receive them, and ye shall have them."

Hebrews 13:8 reminds us that Jesus Christ is the same yesterday, and today, and forever. God's pattern for seeing Jesus will always be the same. Another truth is that what He has done for others, He will do for you!

John 14:6 says, "Jesus saith unto him, I am the way, the truth, and the life: no man *cometh* unto the Father, but by Me." The Greek word cometh is *erchomai,* expressed as: appear. So if we come (appear) to the Father, we will see Jesus!

John 16:24 says, "Hitherto have ye asked nothing in My name: ask, and ye shall receive, that your joy may be full."

Jesus Will Appear to Multitudes Before the Rapture!

I believe that Jesus will appear to multitudes before the Rapture. I believe this because of the following experience. Recently I was teaching some of this material in the church that Donna and I pastor, and the Lord spoke to me saying, "I am going to start appearing to people more often just before the Rapture. In fact, I am going to start appearing to crowds of people and teach them, just before the Rapture!"

When the Lord spoke this information to me, my mind started working like a computer searching for Scriptures to support this announcement.

Here are the Scriptures I found: After Jesus died and rose from the dead, He appeared to the eleven disciples, a group of people, and taught them (see Mark 16:14-19). Jesus also taught the apostles that He had chosen for 40 days after He had risen from the dead (see Acts 1:2-9). And He was seen by 500 at once (see 1 Cor. 15:6).

As you study Joel 2:23, you will find God saying that all of the great manifestations of God that have ever taken place from the beginning of time and all of the manifestations of the present times will again happen in the last days. Note too that the rains of God are in reference to His blessings. Matthew 5:45 says, "your Father which is in heaven:

for He maketh His sun to rise on the evil and on the good, and sendeth *rain* on the just and on the unjust."

Also notice in Joel 2:28 how in the last days God will pour out His Spirit and there will be dreams and visions.

So everything God has done in the past, He will do in the last days; dreams and visions will be part of this outpouring.

Jesus appearing to people 2,000 years ago is the rain of the past. Acts 2:17-21 repeats Joel 2, just using other words.

Look at First Peter 1:5, "Who are kept by the power of God through faith unto salvation ready to be revealed in the *last time.*" Note that the phrase "unto salvation" is one word in the Greek, which is *soteria.* However, the root word for *soteria* is the Greek word *soter.* This word is coequally rendered as: Christ, Savior.

The phrase, "to be revealed" is one Greek word *apokalupto.* The fuller meaning of this word in the Greek is: to make known, make manifest, disclose which before was unknown.

The Greek word for last in this passage is *eschatos* also rendered as: end, final. And the Greek word for time in this passage is *kairos, meaning* an occasion, set or proper time, season, year. So let's put the fuller Greek meanings in this verse to get a little bit clearer meaning of First Peter 1:5: Who are kept by the power of God through faith *Christ our Savior* ready to make manifest what was unknown; in the final *end season and year.*

It is very clear; Jesus is going to appear in the last seasons or years! And I believe we are there!

Ephesians 5:27 says, "That He might present it to Himself a glorious church...." The phrase, "a glorious" is one word in the Greek, *endoxos*. The foundational word is *doxa* and it is coequally rendered as, "the reputation." And the word in this passage, church, throughout the Word of God, is in reference to the Body of Christ (see Eph. 1:22-23; the Church, which is His body, the fullness of Him). When the Rapture takes place, there will be a people (the Church that includes Christians worldwide) who will have the reputation of Jesus! If you have the reputation of Jesus, I believe you will certainly have the ability to see Jesus.

First John 3:2 says when He shall appear, we shall be like Him! If we are like Him, we certainly will be able to see Him!

CHAPTER 14

Testimonies of Jesus Appearing

In this chapter are three testimonies of people who had the experience of Jesus appearing to them after they heard my teaching about how Jesus wants to appear to people. They either heard by sitting under my teaching, listening to a CD, or watching the video of this teaching from our Website.

The purpose of this chapter is to show that faith comes by hearing, and hearing by the Word of God (see Rom. 10:17). It is also meant as an encouragement in seeking your own appearance from Jesus.

I have been pastoring and conducting crusades in other countries on a full-time basis since 1972, and I've witnessed that Romans 10:17 is so true. People will have faith to do what they have been taught. If people are not taught about the great blessing that comes to a person's life when they are filled with the Holy Spirit and speak in tongues, people will not receive this wonderful gift of tongues. If people are not taught healing, they will never receive healing. If people are not told about financial prosperity, they will not be prosperous.

That is the reason I have written this book, so people will have faith to have Jesus appear to them, so they too can have divine inspiration from God.

If people are taught by the Holy Scriptures that Jesus wants to appear to them and they are given the simple Bible pattern and doctrine, people will then have visions and appearances of Jesus. I believe this is going to be a normal thing for people of the last days.

In fact, as shared previously, the Lord recently spoke to me and said in the last days He is going to start appearing to people in groups, the same way He appeared to groups of people in the New Testament after He died and rose from the dead. He appeared and taught them things from the Word of God. Jesus is going to start appearing to churches in the last days and teaching them from the Word of God.

Here are a few passages that give validity to Jesus' appearing to groups of people after He had died and rose from the dead. Keep in mind that we today are of the same dispensation.

In Matthew 28:1-10 there is the story of Jesus appearing to Mary Magdalene, Mary the mother of James, and Salome (see Mark 16:1) and giving them instructions.

In Mark 16:12-13 and Luke 24:13-35, Jesus appeared to two disciples and inspired them and taught them.

In Luke 24:36-48 and John 21, Jesus appeared to His disciples and inspired them and gave them the powerful

New Testament teaching for which He paid for on the cross. This is the position Christians have as a chosen generation, a royal priesthood (see 1 Peter 2:9). And now we have the divine right to remit. The Greek word for remit in this passage is *aphiemi,* meaning: forgive, forsake, omit (send) away people's sins. Also notice First John 5:16.

Because of the price that Jesus paid, we have the authority to forgive people's sins. The only sin we cannot ask God to forgive is "the sin unto death," which is the sin of rejecting Jesus Christ as Lord or the blasphemy of the Holy Spirit.

The God-given purpose of us forgiving others' sins is this: When a person sins, satan then has the right to blind the eyes of their understanding (see 2 Cor. 4:4). So people in sin cannot perceive the goodness of God; and it is the goodness of God that leads people to repentance (see Rom. 2:4). Once the blindness has been removed, it makes it much easier for a person to live a godly life.

In Mark 16:14-18 and John 20:26-29, Jesus appeared to His disciples and gave them the powerful teaching that belongs to us today of having signs follow us. The Greek word for signs is *semeion* and is rendered as supernatural miracles in the senses-realm confirming the atoning work of Christ.

Also, we have the power to cast out devils! This is the first supernatural sign to follow the believer of the New Testament—that's us today! He gave us the instructions and promise that now we can speak in God's supernatural language. I have a teaching that clearly gives 31 scriptural reasons why every believer would want to and should be filled with the Holy Spirit with the evidence of speaking in tongues (see Acts 2:4).

Jesus went on to say that if we would happen to be in a situation where danger is in front of us (such as a poisonous snake), that we could pick it up and remove it so we and others could be danger-free; and it would not harm us. Or if we happen to drink any deadly thing by accident, or someone is trying to poison us without our knowledge, we would be free from harm.

And we also have the God-given ability to lay hands on the sick so they can recover from their sickness or disease.

Jesus closed this teaching by saying that He would confirm His Word with these supernatural miracles in the senses-realm proving that Jesus is Lord!

I could stop here and still we can plainly see why Jesus wants to appear to groups of people!

In Mark 28:16-20 and John 21:1-24, Jesus again appeared to His disciples and taught and inspired them. Jesus also supernaturally blessed them financially as they caught so many fish that they were not able to draw them in by normal means. God proved to them and us that He will supply until our cups run over (see Ps. 23:5).

First Corinthians 15:6 tells us of the time He appeared to 500 men at one time.

Mark 16:19-20, Luke 24:50-53, and Acts 1:4-9 give the account of Jesus ministering to about 120 (see Acts 1:15) before He ascended to Heaven in their midst. In this account, Jesus taught the people that they could and should receive the baptism of the Holy Ghost, which He promised would come after He left. This baptism would give them the miracle-working power of the God. Notice that in Acts 1:8, the Greek word for power is *dunamis* and is expresses the highest order of God's miracle-working power.

The following are the testimonies of Jesus appearing to others:

Testimony of Leoni M., Houston, Texas

Hi Pastor Mel,

I listen to all your podcasts and watch you on YouTube. You have also been very helpful to me on several occasions in regards to spiritual warfare and other questions I had. But today I am writing as you have requested; that if we listened to your teaching, which was "Jesus wants to appear to you" and it happens, we should write with our testimony.

Well, I have been "cleaning house" and decided to clean my whole house from everything that might not be God-ordained and that might offend the Holy Spirit. I just wanted everything to be clean and holy, so that the Holy Spirit would feel welcome.

Every now and then, I would pray, and say, "Jesus, if I have overlooked something, please show me."

So the other night, I was half awake and half asleep, but what woke me was an incredible, powerful feeling over my whole body—it was sort of like an electric shock. Then I felt the wind. Incredible strong wind in my face. I could hear the noise of the wind in my ears. I think I was trying to catch my breath, as it felt like it was almost blown out of my lungs!

And there before my eyes, I saw what I think was the pit of hell. It was hot, Pastor Mel, I tell you, red hot, I could see the flames, I could feel that heat; and in the meanwhile, I still had this incredible strong wind blowing in my face. The next moment, to the left, there was Jesus—standing there—He looked like the traditional "Jesus picture," long white robe, bare feet, but I couldn't see His face. I just saw His robe, His hands and feet.

Then, "in the spirit" the next moment, I stood in my daughter's room (she is 11 years of age) in front of her little study corner. I was just staring at the desk, but I was not sure what I should be looking at. This part was very clear, being in her room. Then after that, I "stood" before my own bookshelves in my study, and I heard a voice saying: "Leoni, you know."

Then the next moment, I was back in the bed, the incredible feeling and noise of the wind was there, and I was staring into this pit of fire. I called out to Jesus for help, as I could see Him standing there. I was praying in tongues, and then slowly, it was as if there was a giant zipper; the pit of fire was being "zipped up." The shaking stopped slowly, and the wind steadily slowed down, and I woke up.

I immediately knew this was a "message" dream (not sure what you call those), but somehow (just being human), I fell asleep again with no fear (sometimes I have an incredible presence of fear in my room—I was under an evil attack in the past few weeks, and it always comes at night).

Pastor Mel, very early the next morning, I was still half asleep, but I got up, remembered my incredible experience, and I went to my daughter's room. I stood before the study table, looking at the things on the table. There were papers, a science project, pencils, a few toys, books, but nothing really that I would say: *This is it.*

So I almost turned around and walked out, not finding anything, but I stuck my hand out to lift up a loose paper, and there it was, right before my eyes: a Harry Potter book. I immediately knew this is it. (A friend gave me a set of the first 5 books in the series.) Then I walked over to my study, stood in the exact same place as in the dream, and I saw the other Harry Potter books.

Well, needless to say, my daughter and I took much delight in tearing these into little pieces. I explained to her that Harry Potter is not something that makes God happy, and I explained why. She was so amazed by my dream, and I still am, too. I love God so much. I don't want to do anything that hurts Him. I just want to spend time with Him and be obedient.

Pastor Mel, I have been doing your teaching on discerning spirits, but I would *love* to know more. I try really hard to "see" in the spirit, but I guess I need more practice. I know you said *all* of the gifts are for us, but this one is a bit difficult. I listen to your teaching over and over. You know the Bible so incredibly well!! You are really amazing quoting Scriptures. I wish I could do that.

Well, this is my story, "in short"—but you asked we should write to you with experiences, and this was mine. It's precious to me, so special. I'm so glad God loves me.

Blessings,

Leoni M.

Testimony of Janet Y., Troy, Missouri

August 4, 2010

I am confident that this testimony is a direct result of sitting under the teachings of Pastor Mel Bond. We found Agape Church through a divine intervention, which I am positive was an angel encounter. I have seen Jesus once in person and have visited Heaven one time. I am looking forward to this happening more in my life.

Pastor Mel Bond has always taught the most simple, basic concept of the Bible, and this is, If it is in the Bible, it's true and we can believe it. Pastor Mel constantly has stated that, "We should just act like the Bible is real, because it is real." Such simple truths are so life-changing!

Having the privilege of sitting under Pastor Mel's teaching has changed my life. I have witnessed several miracles as a direct result of his teaching. I have a friend who is now cancer-free after five years, who was only given a 4% chance of living for 6 months. My granddaughter is alive and well; the doctors said she had less than a half of a percent chance of being born alive. Then they stated that if she was born alive, there was "no hope" of her remaining alive for very long. My mother is currently recovering from open heart surgery that the doctors said she would most likely not recover from. Following her surgery, the doctor stated that there was "No way she will make it through the night."

I also have seen many family members and friends come to know Jesus as their Savior, people who appeared to be hopeless cases, those you would never think would come to know the Lord. These are the greatest miracles yet!

God is good, He is the same yesterday, today, and forever! With Him, ALL things are possible! Jesus performed miracles when He was here on earth, and He performs them now! All we have to do is simply believe the Bible is true, because it is!

The Testimony of Seeing Jesus

During the course of my granddaughter's extensive stay in the Neonatal Intensive Care Unit in Saint John's

Mercy Hospital in Saint Louis, Missouri, I received a visitation from Jesus.

My granddaughter was born October 4, 2008, at 24 weeks of gestation, and only weighed 1.6 pounds and was only 12 inches long. She was given "less than a half of a percent chance of being born alive" and no real hope of surviving if by some remote chance she was alive at birth.

During the course of her stay in the hospital, we spent several nights praying because she was in such critical condition. The doctors were not hopeful at all and fully expected her to die on several occasions. One night in October 2008, the doctors informed us that her lungs were "overextended," which was a very dangerous situation. They told us that "most babies do not survive this" and that "she may not make it through the night."

I went out to the waiting room and lay down on the couch and started praying. Whether or not I fell asleep or was awake, I'm not sure. However, I looked out into the hallway and saw Jesus walking by and heading toward the intensive care room where my granddaughter was. I jumped up and followed Him down the hall; as saw Him enter the room, I was running behind Him. There were about ten babies in the room, all in critical condition, five on either side of the unit. Jesus walked slowly past the infants, looking in the direction of each baby; He raised His hand over each one while light radiated out of His hand and into the infants' beds.

Friends and family members had been praying for every infant in the NICU and were believing God for everyone to receive the healing or miracle that they needed. Knowing that particular night my granddaughter was in danger of losing her life, I was asking Jesus why He wasn't looking over my granddaughter. As I looked over to where she was, I saw my dad and my husband's best friend standing there looking at her. Both men had already graduated to Heaven before the baby was born. They were both smiling at me and appeared so happy. When I asked Jesus the question, Jesus looked over at the two of them and they looked at Him. Jesus appeared to be in communication with the men, although no words were spoken. Jesus smiled so warmly at them and then glanced back at me over His left shoulder. Then my dad looked at me, smiling and said, "Your baby is fine, He has already answered your prayers. He has seen to it that you will have your baby." I felt such an overwhelming peace and warmth in that room. From that moment on, I knew that Jesus had answered all my prayers. I also knew that He was not upset with me for asking Him about my granddaughter.

The next thing I knew, I was back in the waiting room sitting up on the couch. I don't remember sitting up from the lying down position I previously was in. There is no doubt in my mind that I had seen Jesus that night.

My granddaughter is almost 2 years old now and is doing above and beyond anything the doctors ever thought she was capable of. The doctors have stated that she is "truly a miracle" because "there is no medical reason" as to why she is here today.

Testimony of Ms. Marleen V., Fond Du Lac, Wisconsin

12/20/2010

Dear Pastor Bond,

On October 30 and 31st of this year, Bev, Don, and I were at your church having come from Wisconsin to you for healings, which were received by all of us on Sunday morning, the 31st. November 2nd I wrote to you briefly about this.

I've since acquired your CD and DVD on the gift of discerning of spirits, and your books, *Releasing God's Anointing* and *Understanding Your Worst Enemy*. I've listened and studied intently, and realize I've had this anointing for a number of years; but until now I didn't know how to release the anointing and apply this gift so I could use it to heal others. When the anointing was upon me in the past, I did not know what to do with it.

I journal daily, and the Holy Spirit gave me First Corinthians 2:16 in combination with your mentioned Scripture of First John 4:17, and I've been praying, "I have the mind of Christ and hold the thoughts, feelings, and purposes of His heart." In reading a devotional book I have, the following message came to me: "Look to Me for all that you need and watch to see what I will do." Since then, I saw Jesus in a closed vision, facing me, and the rays of sunlight splendor's healing power flowing out of His hands as He held them out to me. I caused myself to relax and yield to the anointing and let it penetrate my body, and it healed me of a severe tailbone and hip and buttock pain.

I haven't had the problem since.

The city and Fond du Lac County, in which I've lived all my life, has a population of about 145,000 people. I am well-known by many from being a past Parent Teacher Association president and other activities; including church-related positions.

I am not a person who has visions or even dreams, but Jesus facing me and healing me was as real as anything I've ever experienced.

Since October 31st, I have been battling with keeping my healings. Whenever I voice them openly, all symptoms would return, yet I have been able to "get my healing back," and I actually can't recall ever being so healthy. I'm 68 years of age, and I am on Medicare and they have questioned the fact that its year-end and my deductible hasn't been met yet; they asked, Don't you ever go to the doctor? Aren't you ever sick? No! Last week I had a sinus cold come upon me and in two days, through communion (which I take daily) and God, it was healed; no doctor, no prescriptions or medications. I don't even go that route.

I pray all of God's special blessings and anointing to continue to flow abundantly in your life and your walk with the Lord. Thank you for helping others to help others through your many talents and gifts.

Blessings to you and all those you love!

Respectfully yours,

Marleen

CHAPTER 15

Galatians 1:8

Galatians 1:8 says, "But though we, or an angel from heaven, preach any other gospel unto you than that which we have preached unto you, let him be accursed."

Before you begin this chapter, I want to say that you never have to be afraid of being used or fooled by a demonic spirit if you follow these simple, child-like rules regarding a supernatural experience. Number 1, make sure there are *at least three clear Scriptures* to validate the supernatural happening is of God. Jesus said to let every word be established in the mouth of two or three witnesses (see Matt. 18:16). The word *word* in this passage is the Greek word *rhema*, which is coequally rendered as, "command, matter or topic"; all of God's commands, matters, or topics or doctrines. God's commands are things that are solid, that cannot be refuted; God's commands will never pass away, and they will never change.

Number 2, make sure there is *no fear* involved with the experience at all. Second Timothy 1:7 clearly teaches that

God does not give us the spirit of fear, but of power and of love, and of a sound mind.

Number 3, you need to answer the question, *Who does it glorify?* The supernatural experience must glorify God! Jesus was teaching about the Holy Spirit coming to take His place after He left this world in John 16:12-14, "I have yet many things to say unto you, but ye cannot bear them now. Howbeit when He, the Spirit of truth is come, He will guide you into all truth: for He shall not *speak* of Himself; but whatsoever He shall hear, that shall He speak: and He will shew you things to come. He shall glorify Me: for He shall receive of Mine, and shall shew it unto you."

Second Corinthians 2:11 says, "Lest Satan should get an advantage of us: for we are not ignorant of his devices." A device is like a large vice that a mechanic uses to hold things in place so it is totally under his control. The devil has devices (vices); and if he gets us in his vice, he will control us at his will (see 2 Tim. 2:26). And the devil's will is to kill, steal and destroy (see John 10:10).

The purpose of this chapter is to warn you to be cautious not to open yourself up to the demonic realm. If you open yourself up to the spirit world to be used by the gifts of the Holy Spirit, the demons of hell understand what you are doing because they live in the spirit world also. And they will try to manifest themselves to you. If you do not know the difference between an angelic and a demon spirit, you could be used unrighteously. Both the godly realm and the satanic realm are spiritual, and both are supernatural.

For instance, a fortune teller or a necromancer or a clair-voyant or a wizard or a witch open themselves up to the spirit world to hear voices or see spirits; demons in the spirit world then communicate with them.

Familiar spirits are demon spirits that are familiar with a person. This familiar spirit knows things that a person has done or where a person has been, and some secrets that only that person would know, even what a person looks like, their habits. These demonic, familiar spirits are very famil-iar with a person's voice, and they have the ability to imitate that voice to fool people. Again, very supernatural, but very demonic.

When people open themselves to the demonic world, a familiar spirit can speak and reveal things supernaturally (supernatural, yes; of God, absolutely *not)* to them. If peo-ple do not know the difference between God's voice and the voice of a demonic spirit, they could get caught in a very demonic trap.

Let's examine an account in the Bible that shows what I am talking about. Look at First Samuel 28:3-12:

Now Samuel was dead [Samuel was the prophet of God that God's people went to, to get direction from God. Samuel knew how to hear the voice of God]....
And Saul had put away those that had familiar spirits, and the wizards, out of the land. ...when Saul saw the host of the Philistines, he was afraid and his heart greatly trembled. And when Saul enquired of the Lord, the Lord answered him not, neither by dreams, nor by Urim [the High Priest], *nor by prophets. Then said Saul unto his*

servants, Seek me a woman that hath a familiar spirit, that I may go to her, and enquire of her. ...And Saul disguised himself...and went and...came to the woman by night: and he said, I pray thee, divine unto me by the familiar spirit, and bring me him up, whom I shall name unto thee. ...he said, Bring me up Samuel. And when the woman saw Samuel....

People used by familiar spirits or any other demonic office do not have the power or ability to bring a person's spirit into manifestation who has died. What happens is a demonic familiar spirit is manifested and imitates the dead person's voice, appearance, mannerism, some of their knowledge, etc. It is very supernatural, and very demonic.

God's Gifts Versus Satan's Counterfeits

For everything that God has that is pure, holy, and accurate, satan has a counterfeit. Again, you can divide the two extremely easily, by using the three guidelines mentioned: two or three Scriptures to support the experience; no fear; and answering the question: does it glorify God?

It is important that you understand what I am talking about to help you avoid satan's deception. Let's compare some of God's gifts to satan's influences.

God's Word, God's prophets, and the gift of the Word of Wisdom give God's people insight into the future.

The devil's counterfeit is a person under the demonic influence of a fortune-teller. The fortune-teller hears the voice of a demon or receives a demonic perception. These demons are really just familiar spirits and have no ability at all to know the future. However, they can be familiar with people and things and say some things that would be accurate along those lines to deceive people.

What about God's prophets and a person of God who knows how to flow with the gift of the discerning of spirits versus the demonic office of a necromancer? God's prophets and the gift of discerning of spirits see into the spirit world; and at times God will allow them to see someone who has died. For example, Jesus saw Elijah with Moses: and they were talking with Jesus (see Mark 9:4).

A person who is used by a demonic spirit of necromancy professes to have the ability to communicate with the dead, but they actually communicate with familiar spirits. These familiar demon spirits are familiar with people, places, and things; so they communicate this information to the person in that demonic office.

However, demons are liars, and great deceivers. They will use those people for the demons' gain somehow. And they will not always be accurate, because they are liars and deceivers. They will make a fool out of that person many times, because demons kill their own.

God's prophets and people who flow with the gift of discerning of spirits can see into the spirit world. People under the demonic influence of clairvoyance say they also see into the spirit world—and they do, but all they see are demons.

I don't capitalize the word satan, and here's why. In First Corinthians 2:6, the Bible tells us what Jesus did to satan when He (Jesus) hung on the cross for all of humanity's sins and then was raised from the dead. Verse 6 says, "nor of the princes of this world, that come to naught." The Greek word for naught is *katargeo,* meaning useless, abolish, vanish, make void.

And in Colossians 2:14-15, "...nailing it to His cross; and having spoiled principalities and powers, He made a shew of them openly, triumphing over them in it [on the cross]."

If satan has been abolished, if he is now useless and is vanished, then he is not a person, place, or a thing—he is *nothing!* In the English language, we don't capitalize names of nothings.

My Experience

I want to share an experience to bring out the fact that supernatural spiritual experiences happen—but they are not all of God. It is vital that we know the difference, so we are not deceived.

Second Corinthians 11:14 says, "And no marvel; for Satan himself *is transformed* into an angel of light" The phrase "is transformed" is the Greek word *metaschematizo,* which is translated as: disguise.

It was about 1980, and I was asleep; it was during the night session (about 2 A.M.) when I heard a noise in the house, then heard footsteps coming into our bedroom. Immediately, I sat straight up in bed and in walked three men. The first man and the third man were dressed the way men dressed in the days of Jesus, and the second man looked exactly like Jesus.

Up to that time, I had already seen Jesus a few times and this second man looked just like Jesus. The two other men were obviously Jesus' disciples. But immediately, I knew it was not Jesus and the two men were not Jesus' disciples. I knew in my spirit that they were demons and it was satan portraying Jesus.

As I was sitting up in bed, satan started walking toward me with his hands extended toward me as if he was going to lay his hands on each side of my head. He said, "I've come to lay hands on you, so you can have my anointing." As you study the Bible you find that the word anointing references a special endowment, a special, supernatural influence or power.

Looking at satan from a natural standpoint, he acted convincingly like Jesus. However, there were two major things that I noticed that caused me to know it was satan. First is the truth in Second Timothy 1:7; there was great fear coming from them and it filled the room. The second thing I noticed: there was no light coming from them. I noticed that there was a dim light that surrounded satan, but it was not coming out of him. These two things came to my mind and spirit extremely clear and strong.

As satan started walking toward me, I immediately said, "satan I rebuke you in Jesus' name!" When I said that, all three started vanishing, and completely vanished within seconds.

A person who is so hungry for the supernatural but is

unlearned in God's Word can be deceived, and deceived so badly it could cost his or her eternal life.

Let me explain with an illustration. A person can be so hungry for a supernatural appearance that they allow their hunger to go beyond the word of God. Then a demon appears to them telling them things that a familiar spirit would know that are very supernatural. The demon spirit says and does things so supernatural that the person follows the teaching of the demon spirit above the Word of God. From this point on the demon spirit leads them to reject God's Word and reject Jesus as their personal Savior. In Matthew 24:5 Jesus said, "For many shall come in my name saying, I am Christ and shall deceive many."

Again I want to say, I am not afraid at all of being deceived; because I follow the biblical pattern I gave you in this book, that will keep you from false doctrines and false demonic appearances.

I am not going to avoid the awesome, supernatural things of God, just because the devil has counterfeits.

Again, I do not want to frighten you. Number 1, God will never allow any kind of a supernatural experience to happen if you cannot handle it (see 1 Cor. 10:13). Number 2, if you follow the simple three steps, you will never be deceived.

Joseph Smith's Experience

In my opinion, Joseph Smith, the Mormon prophet, was a man who obviously was unlearned in God's Word and hungry for the supernatural. On September 21, 1823, he thought an angelic personage appeared to him. I believe this was a demon, and he told Joseph that his name was Moroni. This demon's supernatural appearance overwhelmed Joseph Smith to believe his words. This demon, Moroni, told Joseph that all religions were wrong and an abomination in God's sight, as well as the King James Bible. You can find these statements in the writings of Joseph Smith titled *History of Joseph Smith the Prophet* 2:1-33. This demon supposedly gave Joseph gold tablets that had the pure word of God.

The Mormon religion does not accept the Bible as the Word of God, but adds to the Scriptures by exalting other books above the Word of God. Some of these books are: *The Book of Mormon, Doctrine and Covenants,* and the *Pearl of Great Price.* These so-called "inspired writings" are declared to be of equal authority with the Bible, despite the fact that they not only contradict Scripture in numerous places but each other as well! (Compare Doctrine and Covenants, sec. 132, vs. 1, with the Book of Mormon, Jacob 2:23-24.)

I believe that today we have the demonic religion called Mormonism because a man had a supernatural experience that he promoted above God's Word.

Conclusion

I want to encourage you to read, study, and memorize God's Word as never before. It is the greatest treasure in all of existence. The more you read it, the more you will become spiritually-minded.

Always know that God's Word and His manifestations *are all good,* and they will never change (see James 1:17). You never have to be afraid of being deceived by satan if you follow the simple three steps in judging experiences—and actually everything in the natural or supernatural. Always know that God and His Word are so simple that a child can understand it (see Matt. 18:3).

The entrance of His Words gives understanding to the simple! (See Psalm 119:130.)

But as it is written, Eye hath not seen, nor ear heard, neither have entered into the heart of a human, the things which God hath prepared for them that love Him. But God hath revealed them unto us by His Spirit: for the Spirit searcheth all things, yea, the deep things of God (1 Corinthians 2:9-10).

God has more promotions for you to enhance your life beyond your imagination!

Resources by Mel Bond

Releasing God's Anointing

God's Last Days People

Neglecting Signs & Wonders Is Neglecting the Rapture

Understanding Your Worst Enemy

Heaven Declares Christians' Greatest Problem

Unimaginable Love

Come Up Higher (Donna Bond CD)

Available by calling 636-327-5632 or visiting
www.agapechurch.addr.com

IN THE RIGHT HANDS, THIS BOOK WILL CHANGE LIVES!

Most of the people who need this message will not be looking for this book. To change their lives, you need to put a copy of this book in their hands.

> *But others (seeds) fell into good ground, and brought forth fruit, some a hundred-fold, some sixty-fold, some thirty-fold* (Matthew 13:8).

Our ministry is constantly seeking methods to find the good ground, the people who need this anointed message to change their lives. Will you help us reach these people?

> *Remember this—a farmer who plants only a few seeds will get a small crop. But the one who plants generously will get a generous crop* (2 Corinthians 9:6).

EXTEND THIS MINISTRY BY SOWING
3 BOOKS, 5 BOOKS, 10 BOOKS, OR MORE TODAY,
AND BECOME A LIFE CHANGER!

Thank you,

Don Nori Sr., Founder
Destiny Image
Since 1982

DESTINY IMAGE PUBLISHERS, INC.

"Promoting Inspired Lives."

VISIT OUR NEW SITE HOME AT
WWW.DESTINYIMAGE.COM

FREE SUBSCRIPTION TO DI NEWSLETTER

Receive free unpublished articles by top DI authors, exclusive
discounts, and free downloads from our best and newest books.
Visit www.destinyimage.com to subscribe.

Write to: Destiny Image
               P.O. Box 310
               Shippensburg, PA 17257-0310

Call: 1-800-722-6774

Email: orders@destinyimage.com

For a complete list of our titles or to place an order
online, visit www.destinyimage.com.